GREAT VISION FOR FUTURE

World EXPO 2010 Shanghai

CONTENTS

Shanghai EXPO 2010 Australia Pavilion Competition

Project name: Australia Pavilion Proposal **Designer:** Tonkin Zulaikha Greer Architects **Place in the competition:** Entry to the final **Organiser:** The Australian Government—Department of Foreign Affairs and Trade

Project Description:

The Tonkin Zulaikha Greer concept for the Australia Pavilion was developed from the World EXPO 2010 theme of "Better City, Better Life". The project team created a story for the Australian Pavilion called "Southern Skies, Australian Stories". This tells of the Australian people in contemporary urban environments and informed the design of three design solutions. The story was based on the idea that the most captivating way to promote Australia in China is through the personality and lifestyle of its inspirational people.

From a distance, the Australia Pavilion is a bold statement in form and pattern. It is sited proudly between its neighbouring countries in Oceania, but like the nation itself, is centred between the larger European, American and Asian blocks.

Internally, careful planning and space layout were designed to accommodate a very high expected visitation. From the developed queue experience, an integral and entertaining part of the pavilion visit, through the Southern Skies Performance Area, along the Australian Stories journey to the innovative retail mix, the visit is orchestrated and exciting. Throughout the pavilion, very advanced techniques of audiovisual presentation based on Australia's world-leading film skills are applied to tell the predominant Chinese audience about their ability to create and enjoy Better City and Better Life.

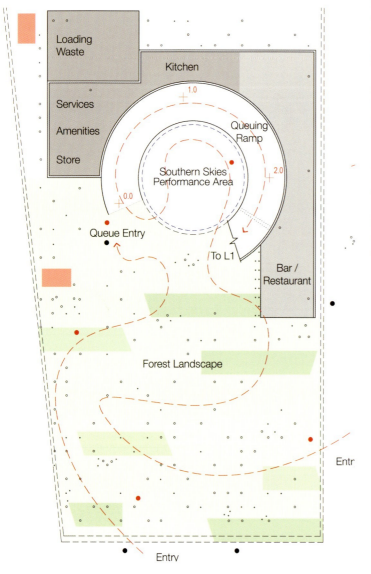

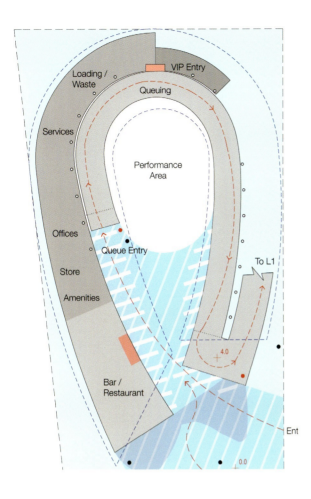

Loading / Waste

VIP Entry

Queuing

Services

Performance Area

Offices

Queue Entry

To L1

Store

Amenities

4.0

Bar / Restaurant

Ent

0.0

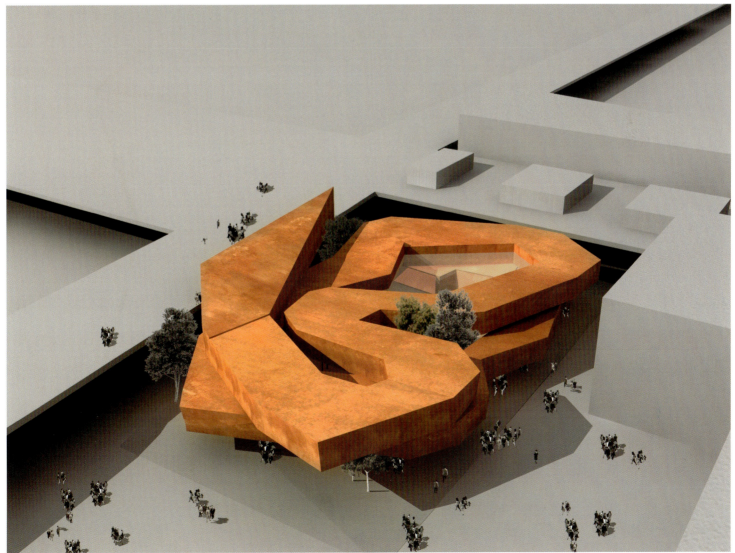

Shanghai EXPO 2010 Austria Pavilion Competition

Project name: Austria Pavilion—The Topology of Sound **Designer:** SPAN & ZEYTINOGLU Architects **Place in the competition:** Winner **Organiser:** The EXPO Shanghai **Theme:** Austria—The Harmony of Urban and Rural Areas

Project Description:

The main driving force behind the design of the Austria Pavilion can be described as acoustic forces, or more accurately as music, music as a concept that reflects continuity in terms of architectural articulation that seamlessly connects the various spaces within the program. The rich history of Austrian musical tradition makes it possible to create a performance program reaching from Baroque Music, to the classic area, to the modern age, to contemporary acts. The space unfurls from within the topological body, from the main space, the audience chamber, to the exterior epidermis. This process creates pockets or pochés that include the rest of the program, such as Shop, Restaurant, Office and VIP Area. Each of these programmatic areas includes qualities connoted with the quality of living within Austrian conurbations: music, culture, culinary expertise, urban scapes, opulent landscapes and lavish foliages.

The pavilion consists of a wood frame structure with a rectilinear roof, no central columns and four walls that seem to dance in a circular motion to become a waltzing box. The building's double-layered skin consists of an inner transparent film and an outer metal mesh similar to a skirt. The predominant function of the building is that of a dance hall for visitors invited to learn to waltz in two minutes with an electronic dance floor to practice before hitting it.

Beyond that the pavilion should serve for various events, including a café, a store and some offices. The classic vienna waltz is a "left waltz", the skirt therefore counter-clock-wise and at the same

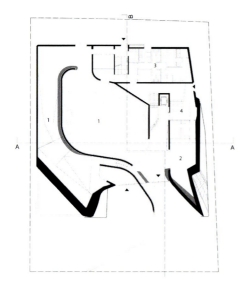

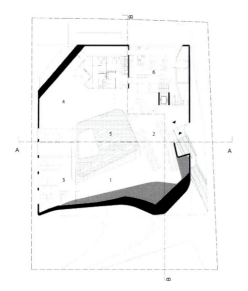

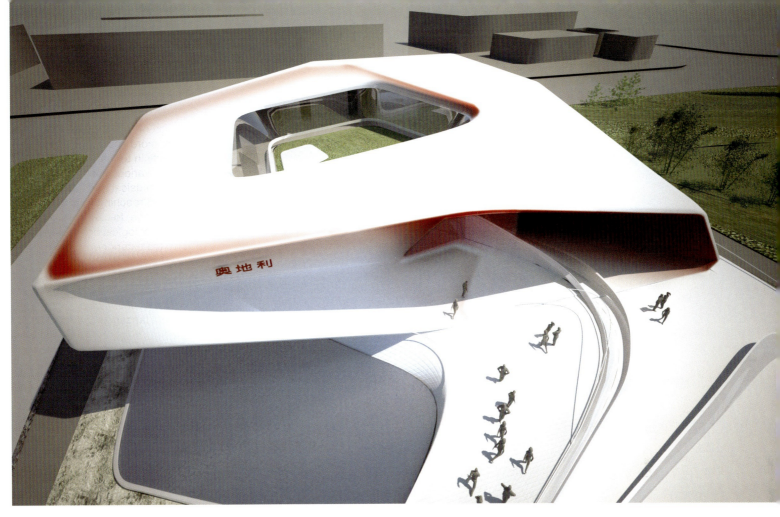

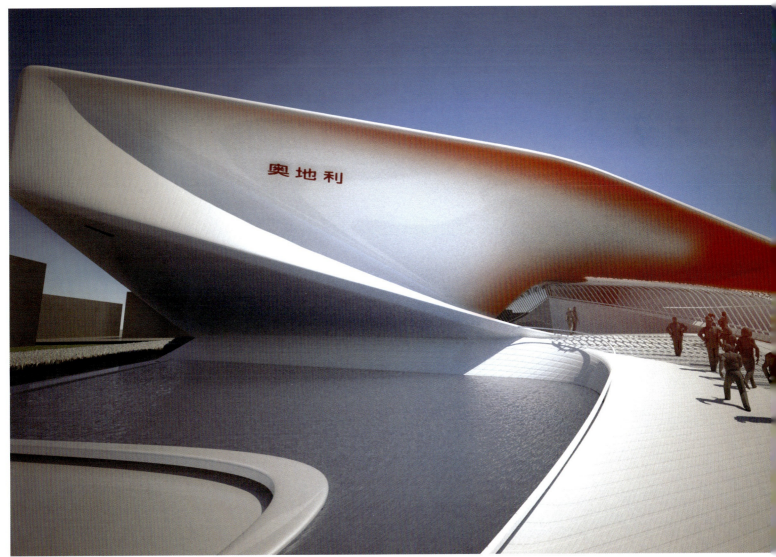

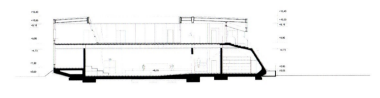

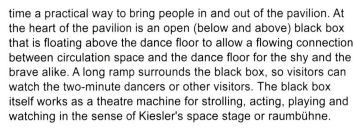

time a practical way to bring people in and out of the pavilion. At the heart of the pavilion is an open (below and above) black box that is floating above the dance floor to allow a flowing connection between circulation space and the dance floor for the shy and the brave alike. A long ramp surrounds the black box, so visitors can watch the two-minute dancers or other visitors. The black box itself works as a theatre machine for strolling, acting, playing and watching in the sense of Kiesler's space stage or raumbühne.

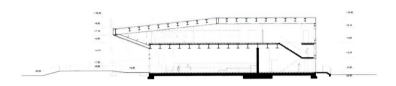

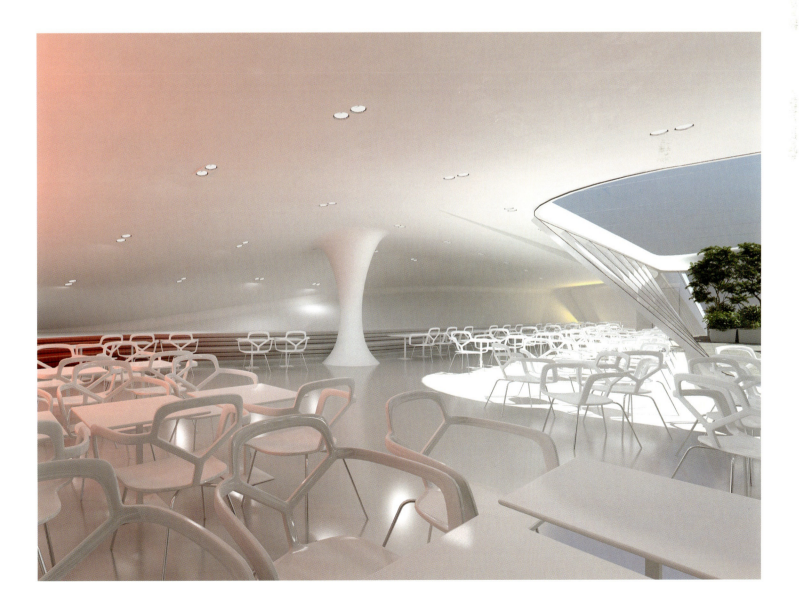

Shanghai EXPO 2010 Belgium & Europe Pavilion Competition

Project name: Belgium & Europe Pavilion **Designer:** JV Realys—Interbuild in collaboration with Conix Architects, Jan Hoet Jr., JNC International, 3E and CJI **Place in the competition:** Winner **Organiser:** Belgian Commissionership for the EXPO 2010 in Shanghai **Theme:** Sport and Interaction

Project Description:

The pavilion is created around the structure of a "Brain Cell", the dominant conceptual image for the building. It evokes the artistic richness of Belgium and Europe, as well as their scientific achievements which contribute to the development and enrichment of their cultural and intellectual patrimony.

The Brain Cell also refers directly to the role of Belgium as one of Europe's main gathering centres and cross-points of three great cultural traditions: the Latin, the Germanic and the Anglo-Saxon. In contrast to the playful, organic and intriguing form of the Brain Cell, the exterior of the building refers to the pragmatism and the discretion typical of Belgium. A big roof structure offers a communal shelter, functioning as a flexible, pleasant and convivial public space, fully open to the outside world.

The changing lights and colours of the Brain Cell will naturally be integrated in Shanghai, "City of Lights". The multitude of visual effects in the pavilion echoes the European Clair-Obscur movement and the Chinese shadow theatre which will be visible from the main public spaces in front of the pavilion.

The pavilion will be composed of a structure which is easy to build, to disassemble and to recycle. To adapt the building to Shanghai's warm and moist climate, the exterior is built up of three mainly closed façades, composed of stretched metal plates. The pavilion does not only accommodate the Exposition halls of Europe, Belgium and their communities and regions, but also offers convivial meeting places, including a restaurant, a bar and a VIP centre.

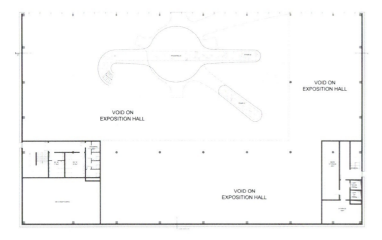

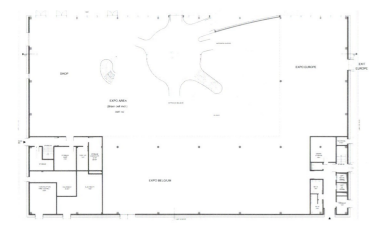

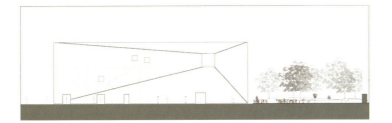

Belgium is a unique place within Europe where different cultures, races and beliefs cohabit, travel and meet. The pavilion wishes to combine this diversity of cultures in a balanced way. This unique combination on a relatively small territory has made Belgium a fertile and creative country, rich in resources and driven by a spirit of openness and tolerance.

Project name: Belgium Pavilion Proposal **Designer:** Julien De Smedt
Place in the competition: Entry to the final

Shanghai EXPO 2010 Belgium & Europe Pavilion Competition

Project Description:
The Pavilion: A Dome Made of Soft Hills

From outside, the Belgium Pavilion emerges through a series of soft hills, symbolising the landscape in the southern part of Belgium and made out of earth collected from minor foundation excavation on site. The hills surround the pavilion itself, interacting with the environment of the EXPO. When snaking around those low hills, one reaches the round outskirts of the pavilion. The discovery of the pavilion is a purely immersive experience. The Belgium Pavilion will function as a journey through various experiences, a loop that guides the visitor through all the aspects of the exhibition content and ties them together to the epicurean programs of the store and the restaurant. A visit to the Belgium Pavilion starts with entering a zone of experiences. The importance of the large interactive space as a visitor's attraction and an umbrella under which all the public functions of the Belgium Pavilion are gathered is intentional and manifest. It is a place for experiences, as it will act as a large screen onto which impressions and expressions of Belgium are projected and linked to Shanghai, in real time.

To Be or Not to Be?

As an international public will see it, the exhibition of the Belgium Pavilion ought to seduce and unite people by ways of coming together around a universal theme, while revealing at the same time the specific characteristics of a Belgium identity. As a country with a unique trans-cultural identity, Belgium itself drives the concept. Indeed, the proposition for the Belgium Pavilion—its design, theme and exhibition—is to be understood in the light of

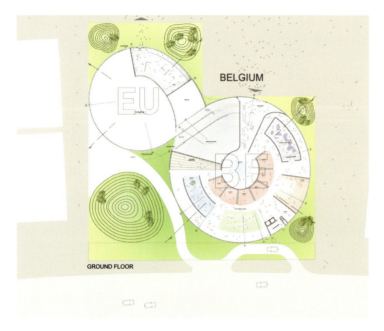

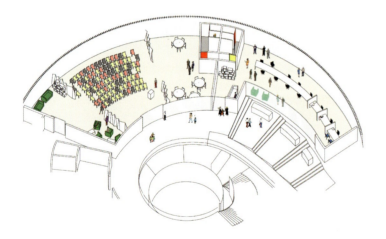

SECTION 2

one typical Belgian condition: togetherness with the others. With a surface area of 30,000 square kilometres, Belgium represents over four different cultures; different regions, communities and languages coexist, meet and sometimes oppose each other. Notwithstanding this patchwork of identities Belgium has also managed to reveal its strength as a rich and renowned tradition for the Arts, an undeniable shipping supremacy, a well-known friendly and rich way of life, performing universities, a dense communication network, artists and sportsmen who travel around the world… By using opposing aspects to produce strength—combining contradictions to create a successful melt, just like the Chinese culture with its association of Yin and Yang—Belgium also proves that by mixing different cultures and know-how, a country or a nation can triumph, be recognised and successful. Territory, different languages, common values and resources, what enables us to define our relationship with the Other? Economy, art, ecology, what does the environment teaches us about the Other? Reflections, shadows, resemblances or dissimilarity, what are the means for representing them? These are the questions that the exhibition will aim at, responding to the prism of Belgium: To Be or Not to Be?

Shanghai EXPO 2010 Bologna Pavilion Competition

Project name: Bologna Pavilion Proposal **Designer:** Performa A+U (Arch. Nicola Marzot and Arch. Luca Righetti) with the collaboration of Arch. Luca Cergna, Arch. Alessandro Miti, Arch. Igor Pilla, Arch. Valeria Roncarati **Place in the competition:** Entry to the final

Project Description:

The design, ideally envisioned for the future, aims to connect material and immaterial culture, intimacy of the architectural space and dynamicity of an urban context, isolation and social networking, the real and the virtual, continuity and discontinuity, personal dimension and collective interaction, planned events and unpredictability. The target is to virtually recreate the individual communication conditions of the everyday life in the so-called "liquid society", simulating the condition of progressive blurring from private to public, producing unpredictable feelings, simultaneously stressed by huge amount of information.

This target is achieved through theme-rooms ("wunderkammer" as we called due to the fifteenth century's origin of the term that means extraordinary objects collection), which are arranged without any hierarchy inside the pavilion. The rooms represent the four motivations that justified the selection of Bologna in the Urban Best Practice Area and the client's requests for a corner specifically addressed to commercial and promotional activities, allow at the same time free use of the in-between flow space. Proposal's complexity derives from the simultaneous coexistence of the exhibition's complementary mode inside each room, which explicitly illustrates the new vision and interpretation of a "wunderkammer": for each of the official motivations—culture and creativity, innovation and technology, human rights and social participation, urban and infrastructural transformations—emblematic objects of Bologna

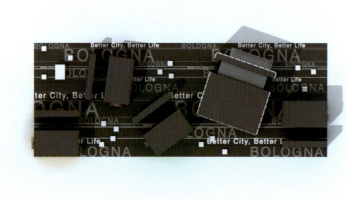

bologna
culture and creativity

Bologna Città
della Musica
UNESCO

area excellence production coexist with short movies about the territory and the production's process, images of the city, drawings and models about the most significant transformations under process, differently targeted publications about the city and the venues.

Image's visionary space interacts with the dynamic and changeable behaviours of visitors, which become an active part of the venues: performance, trade's flows, exhibition activity and multiplying unexpected effects. The opportunity system prompted by the real city becomes virtually condensated and accelerated in the human scale dimension of a "domestic landscape", highlighted by the ultimate design.

ENTRANCE

Shanghai EXPO 2010 Britain Pavilion Competition

Project name: Britain Pavilion Proposal **Designer:** John McAslan + Partners
Place in the competition: Entry to the final **Organiser:** British Promotion Agency **Theme:** Ribbon of Culture

Project Description:

The demountable building would be clad with sustainably sourced timber, some of it from Windsor Great Park, and its central void will be an event space set above a conference-and-café podium. The void, along with the gapped timber cladding, will create an internal microclimate 2–3°C cooler than Shanghai's ambient external temperature.

Eight, a multi-disciplinary design team led by John McAslan + Partners, has created a "Ribbon of Culture" design proposal for the Britain Pavilion at the 2010 Shanghai EXPO. In a collaborative approach, Eight draws on the talents of five of Britain's hottest young practices—Brisac Gonzalez, Carmody Groarke, Nord Architects, Project Orange, and Surface Architects—supported by engineers Arup and exhibition specialists, Wordsearch.

The pavilion's architecture reflects EXPO's "Better City, Better Life" theme. Eight's proposal further develops this theme into a narrative that runs through the building's form, which is based on the idea of a journey through a ribbon of British cities and landscapes. The ribbon rises and descends in continuous loops through the pavilion, which will contain displays on urban and cultural subjects, with airy breakout spaces. "It's a container that need not contain," explained Kevin Carmody, one of Eight's designers. The Britain Pavilion, with its glimpses of British city life and the life of Shanghai beyond, will allow up to 50,000 visitors a day to take a tour through the life of cities in Britain—their history, culture and social and physical environments. It is estimated that up to 70 million people will visit the EXPO during 2010. "The proposed Pavilion is an expression of

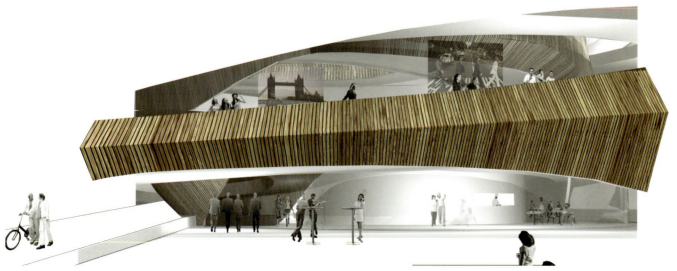

urban, rural and cultural differences, and agreements," explained Eight's Hannah Lawson, a director at John McAslan + Partners. "It's an exciting British can-do building for one of the world's ultimate can-do cities. The pavilion's form and content explain and entertain, conveying a balance between the urban and rural characteristics of British life, and the influences upon it by diverse cultures. The pavilion's key ability will be to suggest relationships, pragmatic and cultural, between cities, and their peoples. It will celebrate our places, our cultures, our commerce and our expectations, many of which will be recognised by the Chinese."

Speaking about the collaborative process, chairman of Wordsearch, Peter Murray, described how the team held workshops to generate and exchange ideas, which were then formalised by the McAslan members. "Whether it's because it's a younger team and they haven't got such big egos, or simply because the chemistry was right, I'm not quite sure, but it was fantastic," he said. "Despite the usual inter-practice rivalry, it worked well." Within the pavilion, there will be permanent and temporary exhibition spaces, with contributions from cities including London, Liverpool, Glasgow, Belfast, Manchester, Birmingham, Sheffield and Cardiff.

Shanghai EXPO 2010 Britain Pavilion Competition

Project name: Britain Pavilion Proposal — UK Network Pavilion **Designer:** Zaha Hadid Architects **Place in the competition:** Participate

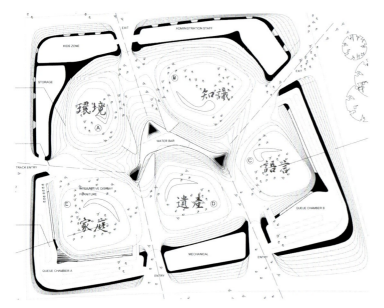

Project Description:

The UK Shanghai 2010 Network Pavilion tells the story of our world's and the UK's world-leading creative, cultural and economic networks in the early years of the 21st century.

The project has been named as the UK-China Network Pavilion because it will embody, and not just display, the kind of networks that are the basis for the 2010 Shanghai World EXPO itself: networks that improve connection between UK and China, and between peoples half a world away, now connecting in new ways every day.

The pavilion is lightweight, low-cost and sustainable. It is a large, open-canopy structure, the plan divided into five chambers corresponding to the five EXPO sub-themes. It is also a memorable spectacle: a structure fusing content with architecture, the individual with a crowd, learning with entertainment. It is a pavilion that creates experiences never seen before in an EXPO pavilion that connects UK to the EXPO's home country, China, in ways that demonstrate the unique position Britain has made for itself in its own unique world-wide networks. From its multi-cultural regional cities, to the Commonwealth, the EU, global finance, exploration, international tourism and travel, world heritage, popular culture, the worlds of science, creativity and the arts, and, most important of all, LANGUAGE – for Britain has got the great stories of the world to tell.

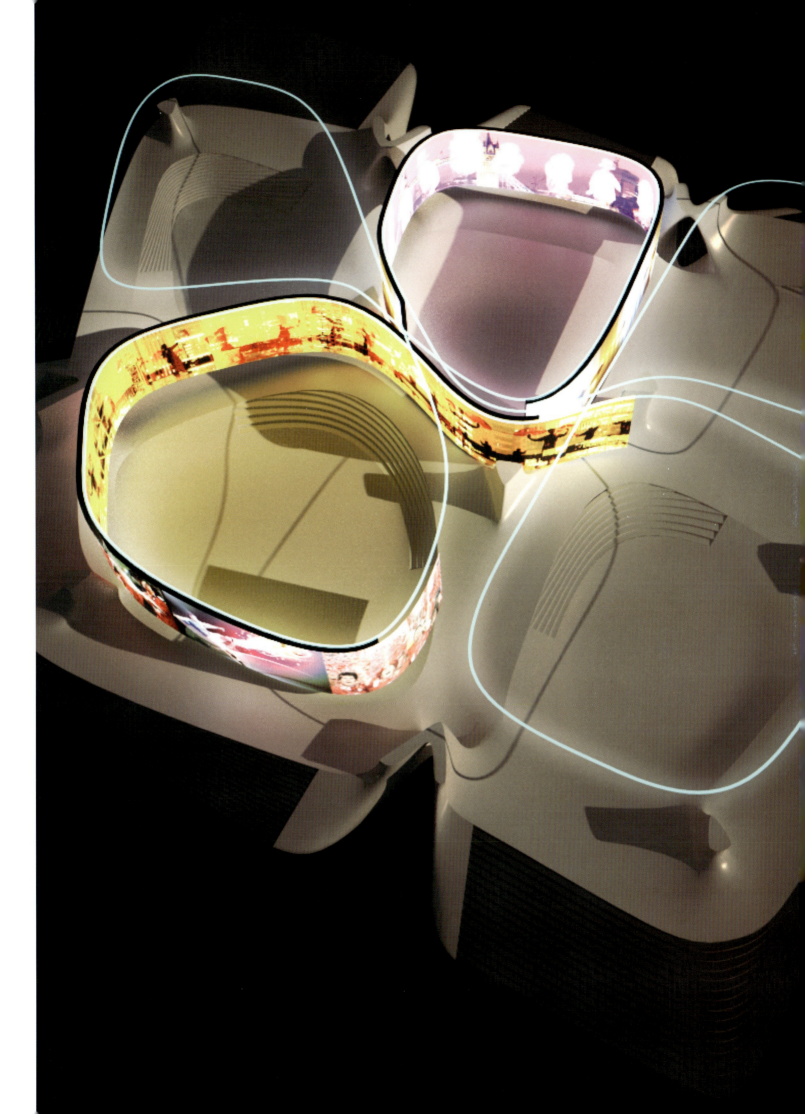

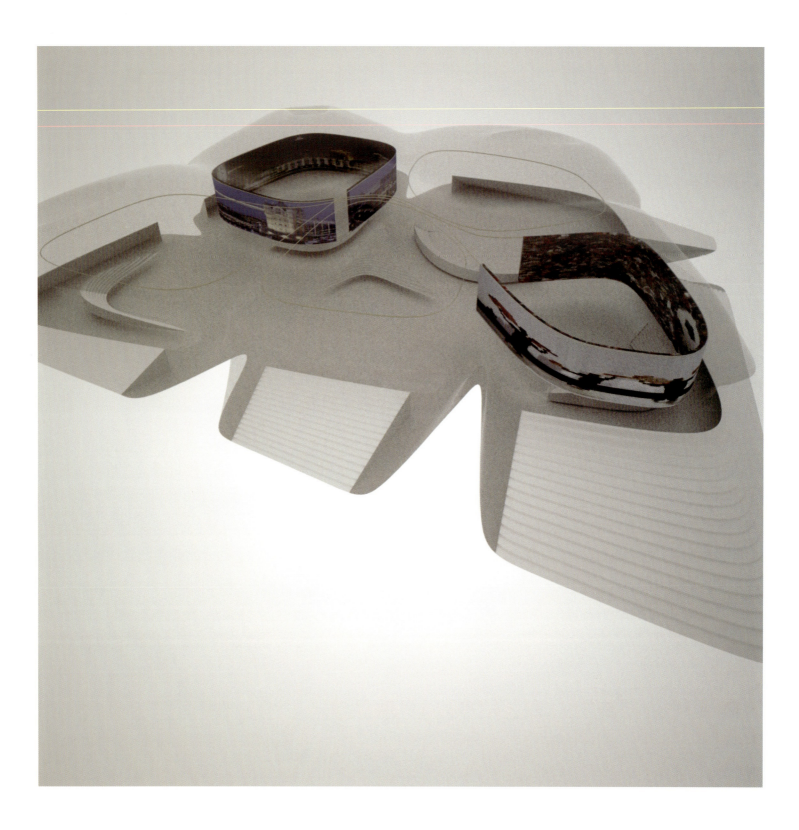

Shanghai EXPO 2010 Chile Pavilion Competition

Project name: Chile Pavilion **Designer:** SABBAGH ARQUITECTOS **Place in the competition:** Winner

Project Description:

Based on a spatial proposal designed to specifically exhibit the pavilion´s contents, the architecture also seeks to take in the requirements of careful representation along with those defined by the program and operational needs of the pavilion. The proposed building is an organic and translucent volume of 2,500 square metres, which hosts in one single big space the different places and premises of the program, considering the ephemeral character of a massive event directed to the common inhabitant of the city in a context of hundreds of different pavilions.

This particular form, along with favouring the purposeful display of the contents, facilitates its insertion in a richly diverse and non-controlled environment, seeking to establish itself as a differentiating element calling out to the visitor. The volume proposes an image of balance between transparency and opacity in a living project that shows and insinuates its content, becoming an active communicator subject to permanent changes in its expression.

Standing out as a single recognisable element, the translucent façade wraps the space, just like the skin of a cell, insinuating the inner public space where the different paths and volumes of the programmatic rooms converge, just like the underlying laws and relations of a fragment of the city. Without a beginning or end, the outer skin and the inner space become one as a fluid and continuous space where the scale and measurements will be given by the users.

The curves and counter-curves, the slopes of the ramps and the

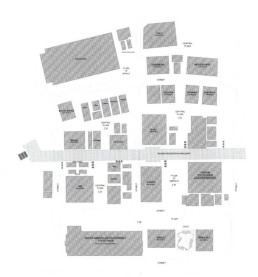

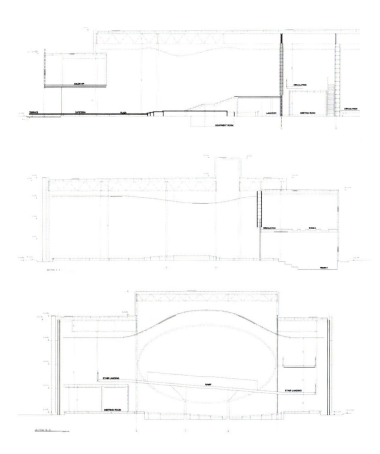

forms and scales of the spaces come alive through the tension generated by the different paths and the strength produced by the meeting situations all generated from the centrifugal centre of "The Seed"; the essence of the proposal is revealed: a vision that defines that beyond buildings, streets and networks, the city is a place for human relations.

The bearing structure of pillars and beams for the enclosure as well as the roof trusses, all of them of bolted steel, favour the assembly and later dismantling of the building as much as a light, playful and translucent proposal can do.

For pavements, ceilings and linings, renewable pine wood, a product of Chilean plantations, has been proposed in its different marketing forms: plywood, laminated and singular wood elements. Laminated pine wood sheets are used as pavement on circulation ramps and as lining for "The Seed". At the same time, plywood sheets are used in lining and flooring of theme rooms and those of supporting program such as meeting rooms and exhibits.

In the main square, a suspended and undulating ceiling made out of steel and wood lattices hangs over a pavement that provides a playful ensemble of different levels produced by distinct lines of plywood sheets cut as ground level curves, providing different atmospheres that favour meeting instances, allowing the realisation of different programmed activities, at the same time, they merge with regular visitor's activities.

Project name: China Pavilion — Oriental Crown **Designer:** He Jingtang, Zhang Li, Ni Yang **Place in the competition:** Winner **Organiser:** Shanghai EXPO **Theme:** Chinese Wisdom in Urban Development

Shanghai EXPO 2010 China Pavilion Competition

Project Description:

The China Pavilion sits on Section B of the EXPO 2010, on the eastern side of the axis, occupying an irregular quadrilateral area. The "national pavilion" and "regional pavilion", as core buildings of the EXPO, would remain there in the future. The national pavilion is designed to correspond to the "Better City, Better Life" theme during the exhibition, with its sub-theme "The Chinese intelligence in city development" as the main content of the exhibition. The regional pavilion will hold exhibitions for altogether 31 provinces, municipalities, and autonomous regions of China, displaying different aspects of Chinese culture and achievements, with its numerous ethnic groups. After the exhibition, the national pavilion will function as a centre for showing Chinese history, culture and arts, while the regional pavilion will be transformed into a standard exhibition hall, together with the surrounding theme pavilions, starred hotels, EXPO Centre, EXPO Axis and Performance Centre, providing a ground for conference, exhibition, activity, and lodging. The China Pavilion will be a symbol in the EXPO in Shanghai, with its huge bulk and central position providing an overlooking view toward Huangpu River and the EXPO area. The design combines Chinese elements and contemporary spirit in various ways, including lifting structure, vertical transportation, red façade, different levels, a garden, and energy-saving and ecological construction.

The lifting structure is adopted to emphasise the theme of "city" and the building as a public architecture, in response to the density of population. The lifting structure makes the pavilion look magnificent

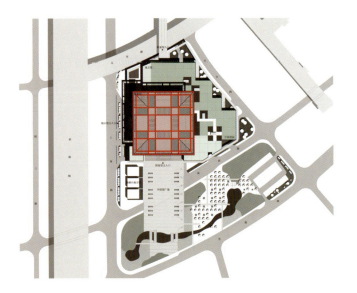

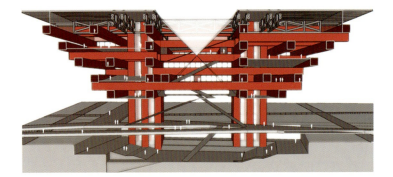

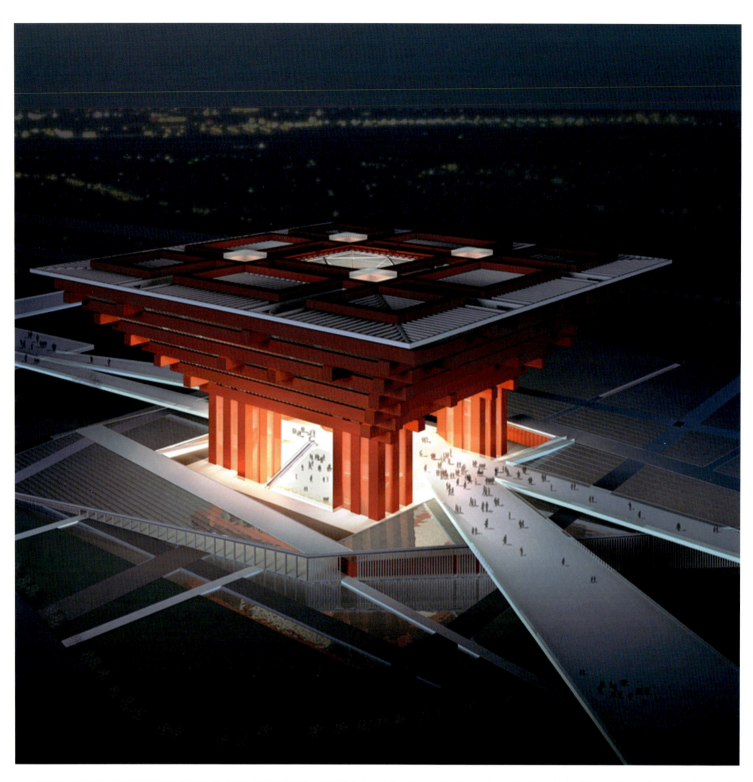

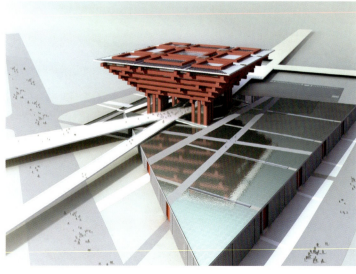

and powerful. The vertical transportation is realised through dividing exhibition areas by different layers. Four transporting lifts move people around among the national pavilion, the regional pavilion and the lifting layer. The national pavilion is further divided into two spaces: the interior and the exterior. Inside there are exhibition halls on three levels; outside, a ramp with good views of the surrounding sceneries is set, and also special speedy lifts for sight-seeing. Thus the needs of functions are met while providing many alternative choices for visitors.

The "Chinese Red" of the façade is carefully designed, with the consideration of "comprehensiveness, strangeness, historicity, contemporariness, configuration and cost", to adopt the material we see now. The colour design is also quite effort-consuming, to take its current "red" as a combination of four different red colours, appearing from bottom-up darker and darker, displaying a sense of layer and space. The configuration with many layers is peculiar, and quite eye-catching. The interior space, divided into many areas, is meant to highlight the flow of space and an interior view without barriers - the standards of a good modern exhibition space. The structure also shows some "physical aesthetics" in modern technological engineering. The roof garden provides visitors as well as citizens with an open public place for joining together. (By Dr. Zhang Zhenhui)

Shanghai EXPO 2010 Pavilion Competition

Project name: Cultural and Trade Pavilions on Northern Area Nord
Designer: Studio di Architettura Luca Scacchetti **Place in the competition:** Participation

Project Description:

This is a general layout for a part of EXPO 2010 northern area, with the design of public spaces, pedestrian ways and landscaping. Architectural project of the renovation of four former warehouses hosts a permanent theatre, a museum, a theme exhibit, and a trade exhibit, for a built area of about 50,000 square metres.

The general landscape design of the area designates a different character for each zone and each group of buildings, but all the drawing is unitary, and all the characters are gathered in a sort of collage in which each portion has recurring themes.

There is a main footpath which connects the main zones and has ideal connections with zones D11 and E05 that stay aside. This footpath is a strong mark, spine and organising axis of the project; it indicates the main directions of routes and the directions of main perspectives. In some points it rises up and gives a sort of theatrical perspective of the landscape, with people moving on different height levels.

The link between the zones is emphasised by the flooring in grey porphyry, realised with rectangular slabs laid down in a random design. This flooring is for main routes, and plays with surfaces in wide and simple concrete slabs.

Other recurring items are photovoltaic street lamps, and water basins in low pools. or fountain jets, supplied by the meteoric waters coming from the roofs.

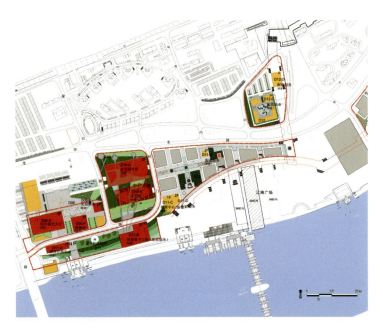

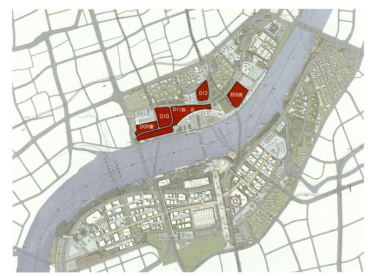

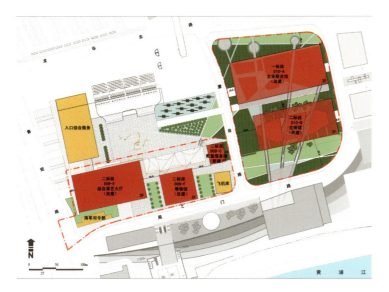

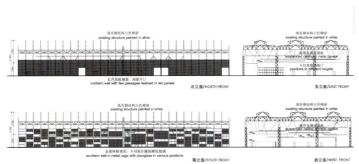

现有钢结构白色喷涂
existing structure painted in white

现有钢结构白色喷涂
existing structure painted in white

悬挂金属屋面板
suspended ceiling metal panels

不同高度的展厅
pavilions in different heights

红色面板墙面，局部开门
northern wall with few passages realized in red panels

北立面/NORTH FRONT

东立面/EAST FRONT

现有钢结构白色喷涂
existing structure painted in white

现有钢结构白色喷涂
existing structure painted in white

悬挂金属屋面板
suspended ceiling metal panels

金属网格墙面，不同部位镶嵌树脂胶玻璃
southern wall in metal cage with plexiglass in various positions

南立面/SOUTH FRONT

西立面/WEST FRONT

Shanghai EXPO 2010 Czech Pavilion Competition

Project name: Czech Pavilion — Urbanised Landscape **Designer:** Film Dekor **Place in the competition:** Winner **Organiser:** Commissioner General Office **Theme:** The Fruit of Civilisation

Project Description:

The Czech Pavilion is built on a concrete supporting plate and has strengthened foundations under supporting peripheral columns. The basic building structure of the pavilion is framed with a horizontal module of six metres. The exterior wall structure is a 50 millimetres thick sandwich board realised by a painted steel plate and a heat insulation material basalt wool.

The basic interior structure of the pavilion is made from steel ribs with plasterboard padding.

The roof of the pavilion is made from 0.6 millimetre thick steel plates situated on steel tie-beams and the heat insulation is realised by glass wool.

The organiser of the EXPO built basic technical and sanitary equipment for the staff and a high voltage and low voltage switchboard on the base plate of the pavilion. The organiser of the EXPO also provided energy supply into the pavilion and at the same time waste and cooling water removal. The supply of drinking water is realised by a pipeline with a size DN50, ended by a closable valve inside the pavilion. Waste water is divided into water used in the toilets and water from the kitchen, showers and sinks. The supply of earth gas also ends near the interior of a side wall inside the pavilion. The high voltage supply cable for the pavilion ends in the main switchboard. The feeder system is a three-phase supply with a voltage of 380/220V, frequency 50Hz with a maximal output of 338 KW.

There is a cooling water supply and removal, with parameters of 6.5 °C incoming water and 13°C outgoing water, for the air conditioner.

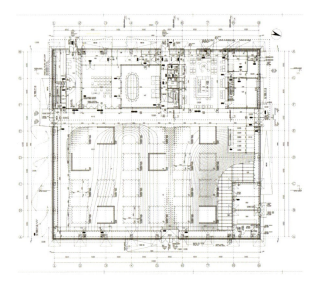

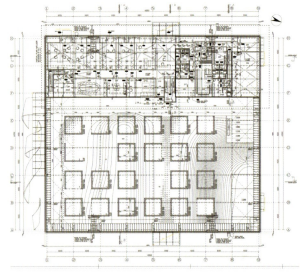

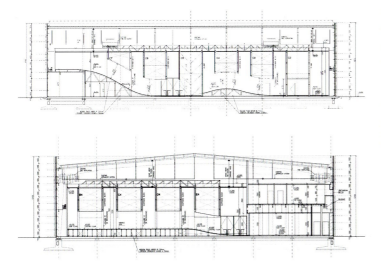

The ideological concept is the installation of 40,000 hockey pucks, which map a part of Prague, namely the Old Town Square. The pucks, as a part of the most favourite sport, are fixed about 12 centimetres from the façade and create a plastic image, during night lit with lights placed on the roof of the pavilion and on the zero level 80 centimetres from the pavilion, causing a light and shade effect on the surface of the façade.

A project named "Ribbon" is linked to the façade, which is essentially a laminate spiral located in front of the main entrance , which serves not only as a protection from the wind, but mainly by means of plasma screens as a basic information system about the pavilion, as well as life in the Czech Republic. The visitor comes into the pavilion with clear and definite information, which will be completed by the mounted EXPOnents.

The doors to the restaurant and the shop are on the side of the pavilion, eliminating the delay of visitors, who only want to buy souvenirs from the Czech Republic or taste the world famous traditional Czech cuisine.

The cornerstone of the Exposition are hanging or standing modules, each measuring four by four metres. The supporting steel constructions are realised by supporting posts and horizontal

timbers. In order to decrease the pressure of the steel constructions on the base plate, the profile of the posts is an H-shape.

Because the essence of the Exposition is hanging the modules and artistic creations inside and the roof has a limited and very low area load, the whole steel construction is self-supporting, including the ceiling from a grid of beams closing the upper part of the modules. The floor of the Exposition is made from cross-beams covered with a desk material, creating an illusion of undulating countryside covered with artificial grass and a contrast with the exact hanging modules covered in white plasterboard. The respective part of the Exposition is directly linked to a "multimedia hall", where the regions of the Czech Republic, will be presented throughout the whole Exposition.

A part of the Exposition is scenic light systems controlled by memory lighting consoles and terminal components—dimmers. Essentially, lights of the profile spot type are used, lighting not only their own EXPOnents, but also creating a basic level of lighting to the EXPOsing area. Lights of the moving head type are used for effective and dynamic lighting, controlled from a particular light console. A part of the lighting park is a superior microprocessor control system, which ensures a time succession of all the attractions and at the same time detects eventual malfunctions of separate systems.

Other systems of the EXPOsing part are electro-acoustics and video projection.

Shanghai EXPO 2010 Denmark Pavilion Competition

Project name: Denmark Pavilion **Designer:** BIG **Place in the competition:** Winner **Organiser:** Shanghai EXPO **Theme:** Happy Life in A Fairyland

Project Description:

The Denmark Pavilion should not only exhibit the Danish virtues. Through interaction, visitors are able to actually experience some of Copenhagen's best attractions.

Both Shanghai and Copenhagen are harbour cities. However, the polluting activities in the harbour have been replaced by harbour parks and cultural institutions in Denmark, and as a result the water has become clean enough to swim in. In the heart of the pavilion lies a harbour bath, which is filled up with seawater from Copenhagen harbour shipped to Shanghai in a tank vessel. The Chinese can swim in the bath and not only hear about the clean water but actually feel and taste it.

The pavilion is constructed as a monolithic self-supporting construction in white-painted steel, manufactured at a Chinese shipyard. Prefabrication will be effective, with an uncomplicated transportation, effective sampling process, rational dismantling and transfer. The synthetic light-blue coating used in Denmark for bicycle paths will cover the roof. Inside, the floor will appear in epoxy, the light-blue bicycle path respectively.

The sequence of events at the exhibition takes place between two parallel facades – the internal and external. The internal is closed and contains different functions of the pavilion. The width varies and is defined by the programme of the inner space. The external façade, pavilion's façade outwards, is made of perforated steel that represents and reflects a Danish city silhouette.

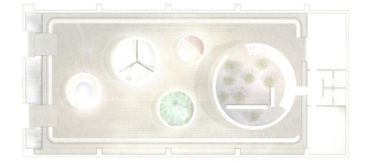

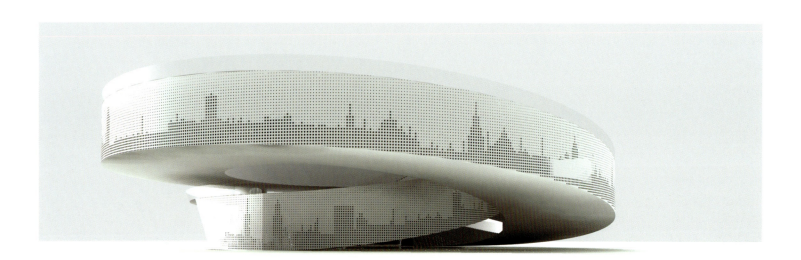

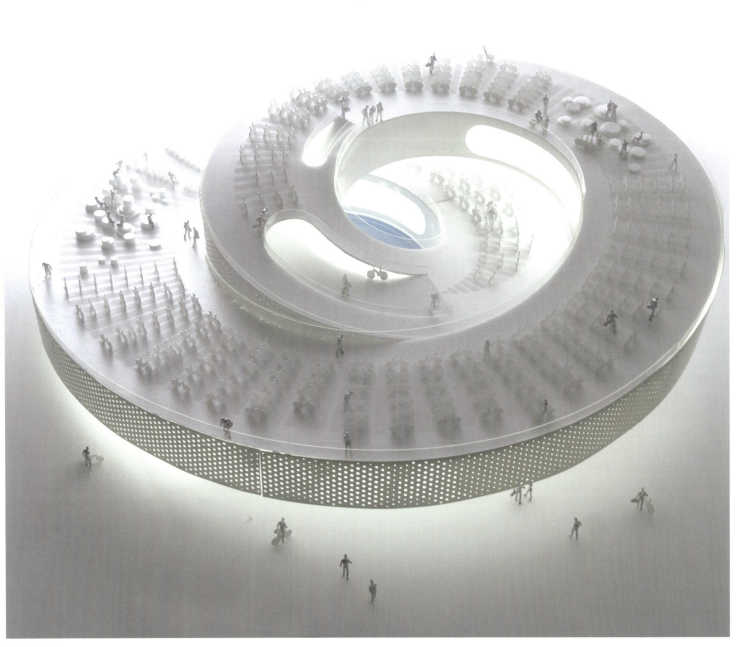
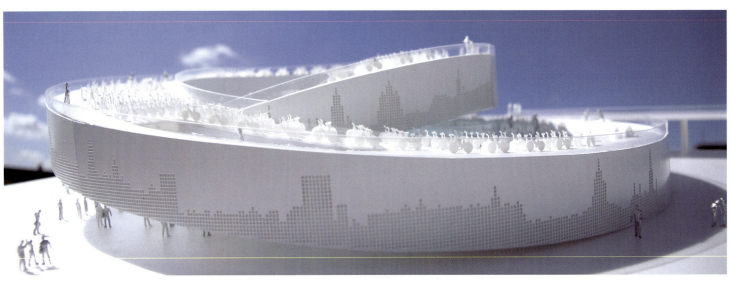

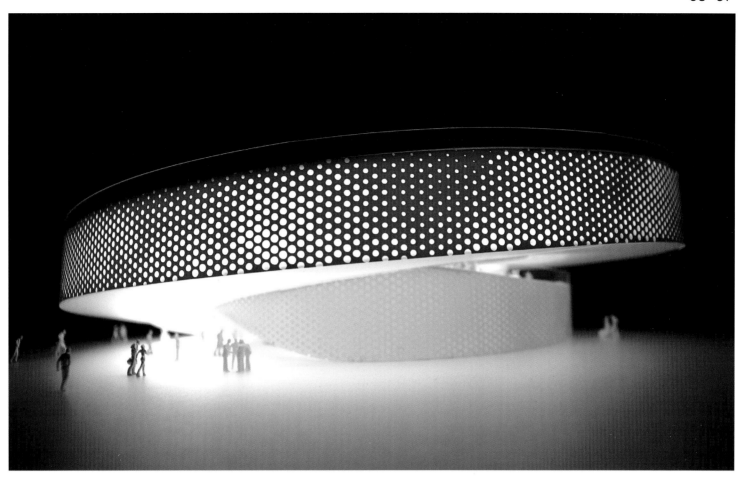

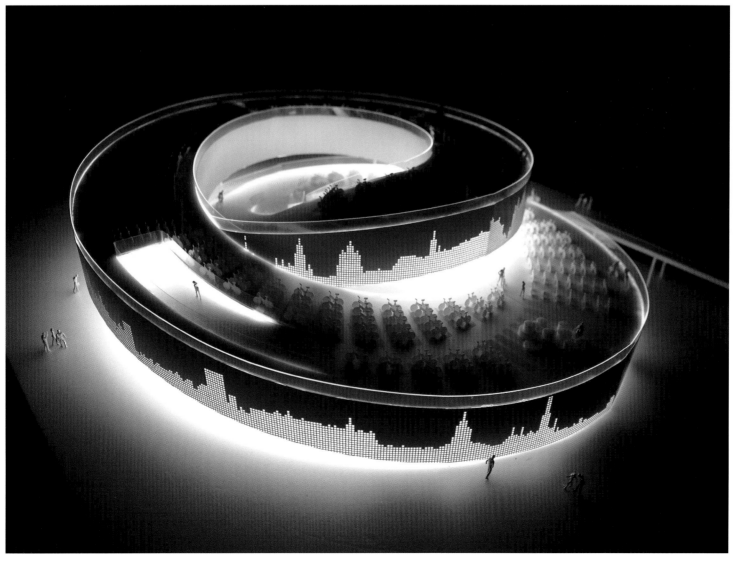

Shanghai EXPO 2010 Denmark Pavilion Competition

Project name: Denmark Pavilion Proposal **Designer:** MAPT Anders Lendager, Mads Møller with Femmes Regionales, KHR and InnovationLab.
Place in the competition: Entry to the final

Project Description:

The EXPO pavilion evokes a new way of thinking about sustainability. It is about mentality! The Denmark pavilion gives the guest the possibility of making a difference. You can interact with the building by loading it with information or by extracting information from it. When you visit the pavilion, your fingerprint is on the building, along with those of other seven million people. Together you can make a difference on a global scale.

The pavilion is a tree-like structure, with a huge digital screen below the "tree top". This is where all information is gathered and shared by the use of RFID technology. Within the top, three different exhibition spaces are located that correspond to the theme "Better City, Better Globe, Better Life." The branching structure creates a light and flexible space that allows the exhibitions to interwine. The "tree top" touches down through three spacious staircases. The trunks of these staircases contain further programmes, such as a restaurant and lounge, a room for press conferences, office spaces and building installations. The structure is designed with top of the line sustainable solutions. The temperature management system uses the absorbed energy from the hot air to cool down the building. The outer layer of the building is covered with solar panels and the structural beams are made from light weight fibre glass. The building takes up the sustainability challenge and translates it into something beautiful. It becomes more than pure survival.

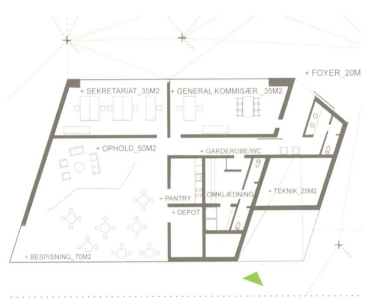

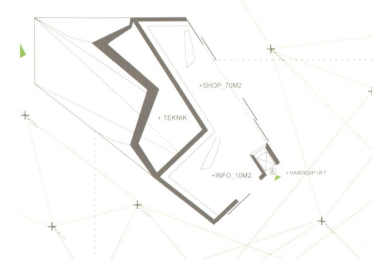

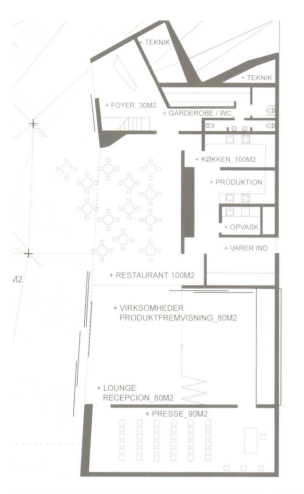

+ TEKNIK

+ TEKNIK

+ FOYER_30M2

+ GARDEROBE / WC

+ KØKKEN_100M2

+ PRODUKTION

+ OPVASK

+ VARER IND

+ RESTAURANT 100M2

+ VIRKSOMHEDER
PRODUKTFREMVISNING_80M2

+ LOUNGE
RECEPCION_80M2

+ PRESSE_90M2

M2

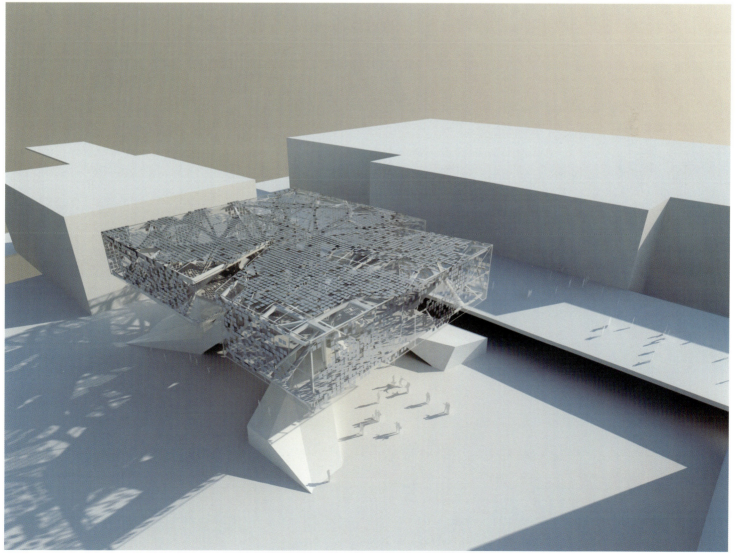

Shanghai EXPO 2010 Denmark Pavilion Competition

Project name: Denmark Pavilion Proposal **Designer:** 3XN Architects **Place in the competition:** Entry to the final

Project Description:

The pavilion is in the shape of the Danish flag on all sides—including top and bottom. The four red rectangular fields, thus, form eight blocks and the white in the flag can be opened in both directions to form an inner square or urban space at the heart of the building. The total volume is tilted slightly to one side, and emphasised in strategic places, thus creating an entrance and an exit that provides shelter from the rain and shade on sunny days.

3XN architects' proposal for the Denmark Pavilion for the Shanghai EXPO 2010 uses their national flag to create a dynamic spatial environment. "An exhibition window is an invitation that says: Welcome inside a little piece of Denmark. And in 2010, in the age of globalisation, it is important to add: Welcome to a Denmark that is part of the world," stated the architects.

Even from a distance, the 3,000 square metres pavilion, constructed with red and white rectangles, is easily identifiable with the Danes. Upon approaching, the building is understood as not only being clad in the country's colours, but also being a three dimensional version of the flag.

Conceptual thinking for the pavilion led the architects to focus on the four areas used to globally market the country: Denmark as responsible and balanced, with a focus on high quality, experimental and courageous, and characterised by environmental awareness, simplicity and efficiency. Each characteristic receives its own rectangle so that the characteristics are reflected not only in the individual forms, but also in the pavilion itself.

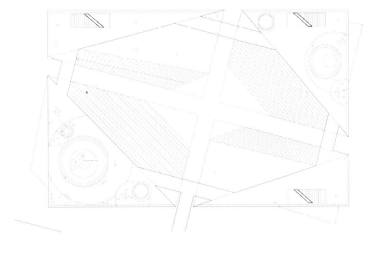

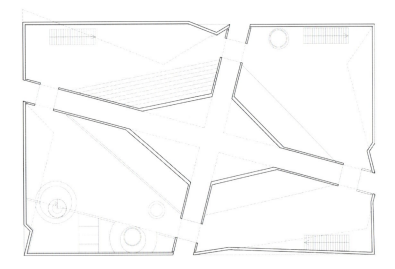

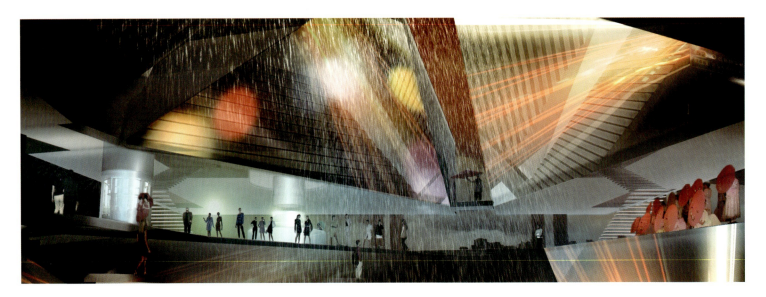

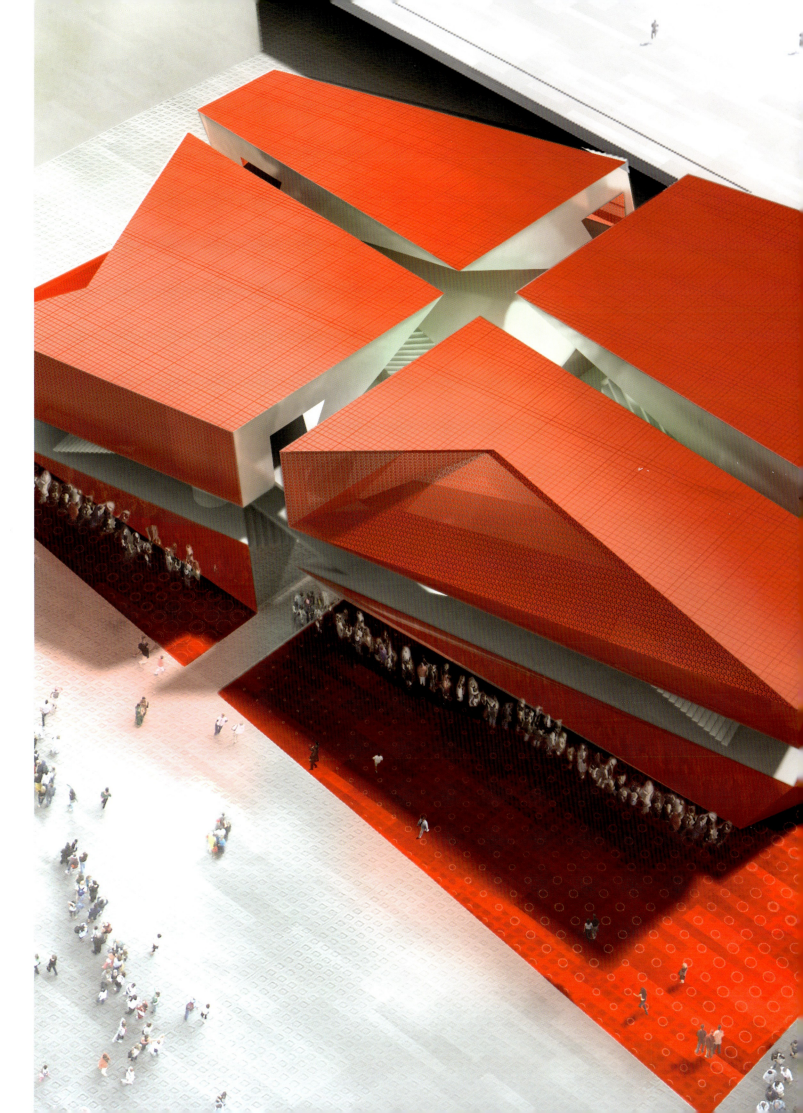

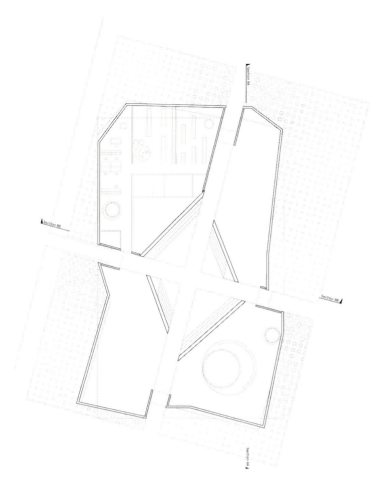

Project name: Denmark Pavilion Proposal — RÉN Project **Designer:** Architec Bjarke Ingels Group (BIG) **Place in the competition:** Participation

Shanghai EXPO 2010 Denmark Pavilion Competition

Project Description:

The work an architect gets to realise in his or her career is the result of random opportunities and chances. Architects can hardly plan their careers, or decide what they want to do, or where.They have to respond to accidental challenges through opportunistic improvisation, mutation and migration of ideas. And often the story they tell is a product of post-rationalisation or hindsight.

The RÉN building is a proposal for Denmark Pavilion, a hotel, sports and conference centre for the World EXPO 2010 in Shanghai. The building is conceived as two buildings merging into one. The first building, emerging from the water, Is devoted to the activities of the body, and houses the sports and water culture centre. The second building, emerging from land, is devoted to the spirit and enlightenment and houses the conference centre and meeting facilities. The two buildings meet in a 1,000 room hotel and form the Chinese character for the word "People", becoming a recognisable landmark for the World EXPO in China.

Together the two buildings become a tower and an arch at once. The arch creates a square for gatherings and activities, exactly on the main axis of the EXPO site overlooking the Huangpu River. The square is sheltered from the rain but allows the sunlight through, from east in the morning and from west in the evening.

Large curved plazas cover the pool and conference buildings, creating a continuous recreational public space along the river. Round openings and roof lights bring light to the auditoriums and pools and become gradually denser as they rise from the river, eventually becoming glittering windows and terraces for the hotel

rooms.
In the spring of 2008, BIG was invited to participate in the competition to design the Denmark Pavilion for Shanghai World EXPO. Upon arriving in Shanghai they were greeted at the airport by the giant blue furry EXPO mascot: Hai Bao (the precious of the sea). It looked strangely familiar…

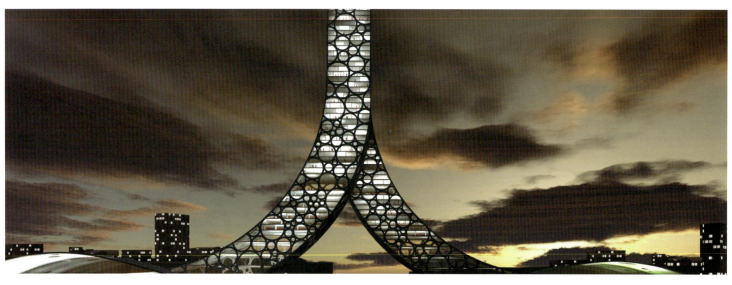

Project name: Finland Pavilion — Kirnu (Giant´s Kettle) **Designer:** JKMM Architects **Place in the competition:** Winner **Organiser:** FINPRO **Theme:** Abundance, Wit and Environment

Shanghai EXPO 2010 Finland Pavilion Competition

Project Description:

The pavilion will rise from the water as an island-like miniature city. A bridge leads visitors over the water into the pavilion, the heart of which consists of the miniature city's centre and a forum for events, "Kirnu" ("Giant's kettle"), where ideas can meet and mix.

The architecture of the pavilion draws its inspiration from Finnish nature. The pavilion floats over water, white and ethereal. The delicate, scale-like surface structure is gradually revealed when approaching the building. A smooth bridge leads towards the entrance, whose warm wood surfaces form a shady and inviting portal to the pavilion. Visitors next arrive at the forum, Kirnu. Sheer walls made of fabric rise towards the sky. The displays and lighting fixtures integrated into the floor create a virtual exhibition that visitors walk over. A gently sloping ramp ascends within the thick walls of Kirnu towards the exhibition hall, a high space that winds around the atrium. After the exhibition hall, the ramp continues downward to the exit, shop and restaurant.

The pavilion's main goal is to present a vision of "Good Life". The six pillars of good life are freedom, creativity, innovation, community spirit, health and nature, all of which have been integrated into the pavilion's architecture, its spatial and functional solutions. The sculptural design represents the freedom and creativity in construction enabled by technology.

A 3D computer model will be created to assist the construction process. The pavilion's load-bearing vertical structures are made of steel. The façade consists of narrow elements, which will be assembled on site. The horizontal structures are made of wooden

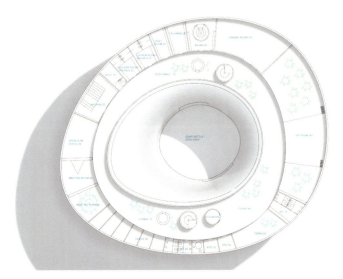

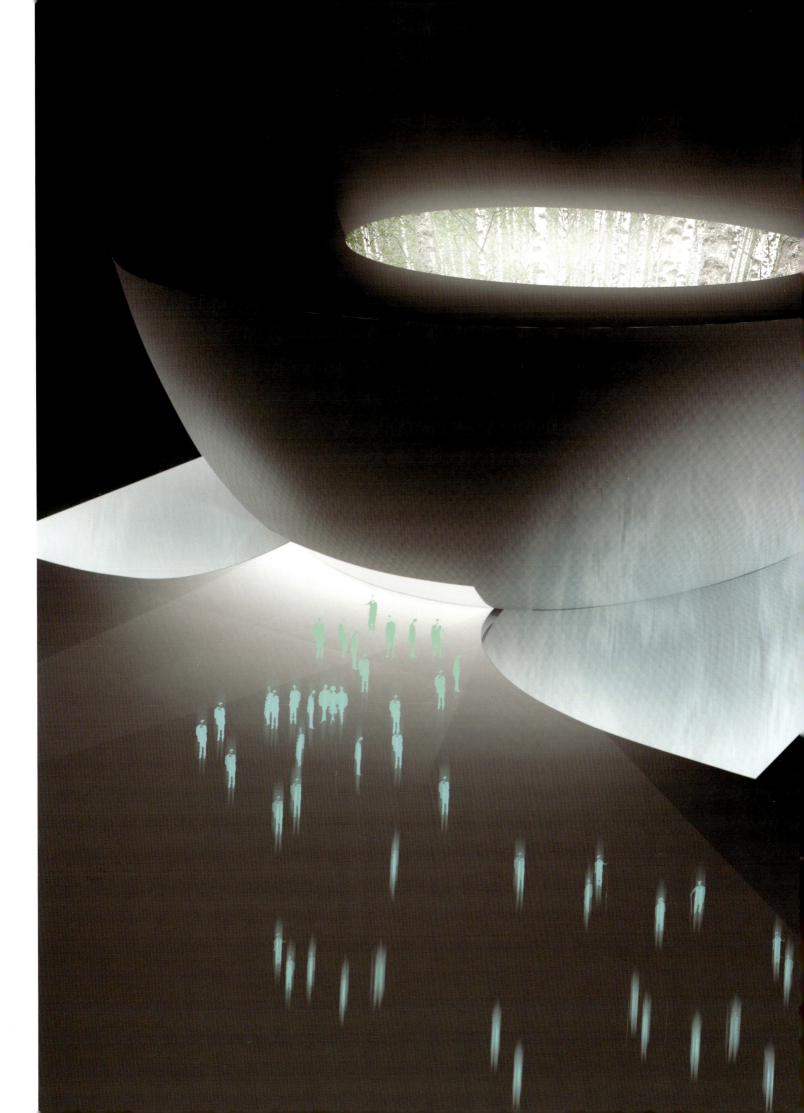

LAPINRINNE 3, FIN-00180 HEL
TEL +358 9 2522 0700, FAX +358 9
WWW.JKMM.FI

冰壶

24.000

elements and the floors of sub-plates. Wood/plate structures will be used for the inner lining. The outer façade will be covered with scaly, modern shingles made of paper/plastic composite sheet, which is an industrial recycled product. The atrium walls and some of the walls on the second floor are made of fabric. The atrium can be covered with a transparent fabric. The stairs and lift will be constructed from individual elements. All of the construction elements will be made in such a way that the building can be disassembled and re-assembled.

The design incorporates, for example, renewable energy sources. Solar panels on the roof power cooling devices in the hottest season. The electric panels feed electricity directly into the building network or store it in batteries. Natural ventilation is used to reduce the need for mechanical ventilation. The supply air can be collected at water level underneath the house. The thick atrium wall forms a natural flue and encases the spiral entrance ramp. Opening wall and ceiling hatches enhance natural ventilation, and the heat stress caused by the sun is reduced by the direction of facilities, the use of light surfaces and the structure of windows. The planted roof can be used to even out the heat load. Rain water is collected on the roof and conducted to a basin in the yard. Geothermal heating is also made use of. The materials are carefully selected so that construction generates as few greenhouse gas emissions as possible. The loading, reuse and recycling of materials will be analysed for the entire life cycle of the pavilion.

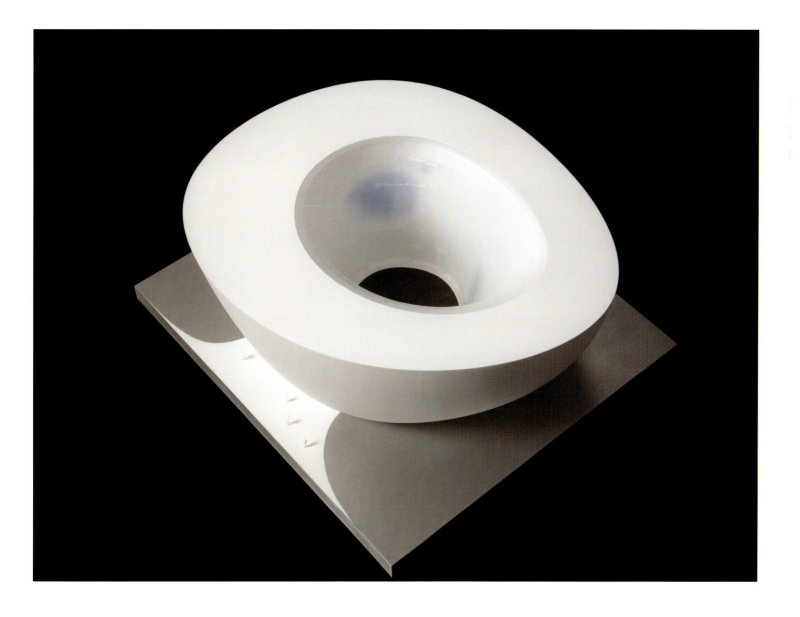

Shanghai EXPO 2010 France Pavilion Competition

Project name: France Pavilion **Designer:** Jacques Ferrier Architectures
Place in the competition: Winner **Organiser:** Cofres SAS **Theme:** A City of Sense

Project Description:

The pavilion appears under a Cartesian shape of a quadrangle, embraced by a thin mineral grid network suspended on a reflecting pool. Lying in the heart of this display case, a formal French garden is placed vertically to create a wholly unexpected planted theatrical setting. The exhibition's way is organised as a gently sloping ramp that circles down around the garden, so that the landscape is placed at the centre of the urban issue. The pavilion is crossed as a space of privileged dialogue between French and Chinese cultures and has a federative theme the "Sensual City"; a place where the six senses exalt—taste, smell, touch, hearing, sight and balance/movement.

A Formal French Garden

The France Pavilion's architecture falls within the "Sensual City" theme. It inseparably combines man-made and natural environments. The garden folds back on roof level to become available to all visitors. Reflected by the water, the building and garden combine in a thousand different ways.

Structural Innovation

Embraced by its structural mantilla, the pavilion rises up above the reflecting pool. The enclosing grid network provides an illustration of France's engineering know-how, with its patterned design simultaneously evoking power and refinement. The grid network, supported over the reflecting pool, is sufficiently raised to provide views through to the very centre of the pavilion and allow visitors to pass below. The geometry is dictated by the rationality of a stabilising structure and the flexibility of a sail rising up from the

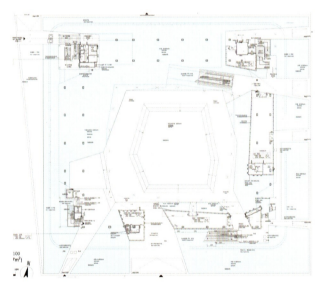

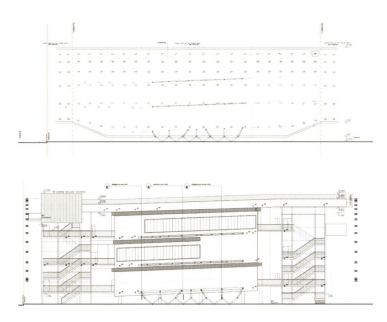

pool.

France receives its visitors in a garden.

The pavilion curves around a large central area. Rising up from this space, a contemporary flowerbed in the form of a vertical formal French garden is reflected in the pool below. The theme is equilibrium, a balance between solid and void, hard and planted surfaces, the rational and the organic. Visitors pass below the grid network and continue along a pontoon just above water level where they are invited to discover a cool universe of alternating light and shade. The bustle and heat of the surrounding exhibitions are kept at a distance; the scents from the vertical garden fill the air with fragrance and the pool's water gives an impression of freshness. The patterns of the vertical flowerbeds provide glimpses of their flower-carpeted rear faces. The time spent queuing in the shade offers a welcome moment of rest and contemplation.

An Architecture of Movement

The pavilion is organised as a gently sloping ramp that circles down around the garden, providing an exhibition circuit that begins at the top and sweeps down to ground level. The reception area gives access to an escalator that rises up to the highest level. Highly visible through the grid network, the never-ending upward flow of visitors animates the entrance elevation.

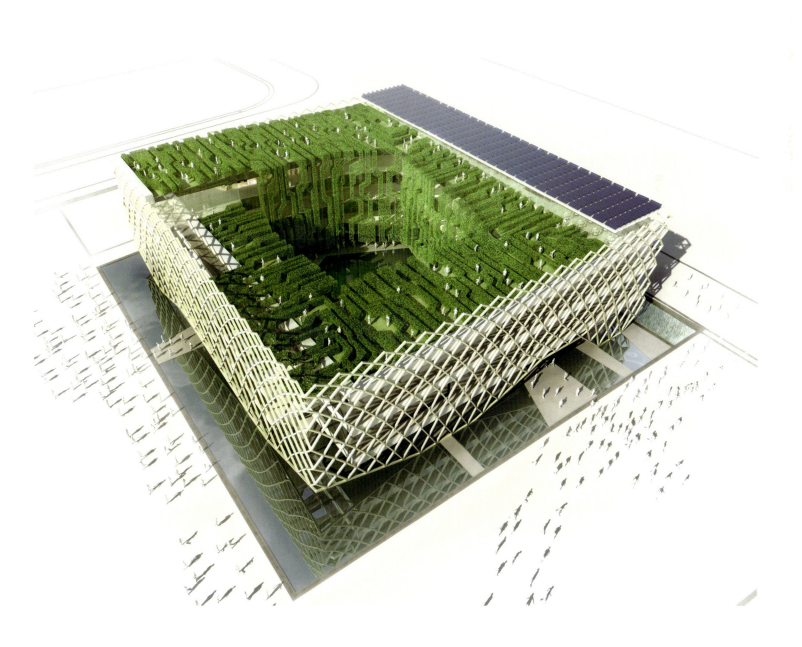

Shanghai EXPO 2010 France Pavilion Competition

Project name: France Pavilion Proposal **Designer:** PERIPHERIQUES Architects **Place in the competition:** Participation

Project Description :

This project brings a number of complex issues into play. To begin with, the idea is, of course, to design a place representative of French identity, a place that serves as a commercial, economic and cultural showcase for France. But it is equally important to ensure that the France Pavilion is an exceptional, out-of-the-ordinary attraction, apt to appeal to and capture the attention of the huge number of visitors (70 million are expected) as they hurry through thousands of square metres of the Exposition area, where all the countries will be vying to offer the most spectacular and captivating attraction.

Before deciding what they wanted, they knew what they didn't want, and that was to reduce France to a single idea or image. They live in a country that is manifold, diversified and specific in many areas, be it in terms of cultures, landscapes, industries and cities. France, as the foremost tourist destination in the world, is a country of crossroads and encounters. It's a place of mobility and interchanges, a country that leans on its history to project itself into the future.

Diversity and mobility are, two interesting concepts to apply to the design of the France Pavilion for the 2010 World Exposition in Shanghai, because they raise key issues of sustainable development for the future of cities.

The theme "Better City, Better Life" clearly raises the question of the role of cities. The diversity of populations, cultures, services, and cityscapes along with the mobility of information, objects, and people in a way that respects the environment stand at the heart of

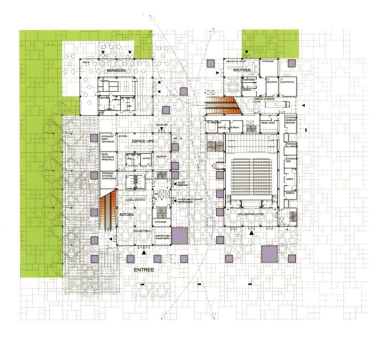

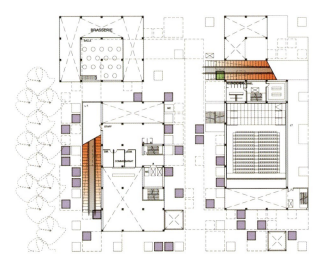

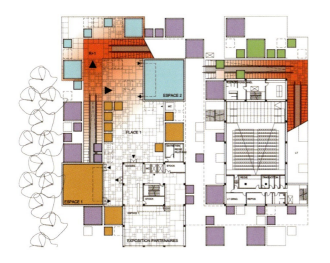

the urban revolution of this new century.

The concept of the pavilion is based on staging a subject and on an open-ended selection of particles and parcels of France, brought together, built up and structured in relation to one another to produce a form of urban architecture in which the visitor is immersed as he/she moves through it.

The importance of the pavilion is to be found as much in its spectacular shape as in the spatial experience of moving through it and the unique nature of the works exhibited.

A design and construction strategy established is compatible with the delays and the budget. The basic principle of the design and construction strategy involves a predetermined yet completely open-ended design on all project levels. This means that the aim is to ensure that the project is never blocked for technical, financial or regulatory reasons.

Therefore, the pavilion is defined as a whole in very precise terms while making the individual components adaptable, replaceable, fungible, etc. A distinction is drawn in the building or exhibition container between the hardware part and the software part. The hardware is firstly the principle of a load-bearing structure, a grid of columns carrying the consoles. The system draws inspiration from

industrial storage layouts. The hardware is also the permanent built components: the entrance areas, the auditorium, the temporary exhibition space, etc. The software is what fills the structure, that is, a series of "display boxes" on three scales: three metres by three metres, six metres by six metres, and 12 metres by 12 metres. Each has its own structure adapted to its scale; the facades are adapted to the contents. Every display box contains a selected particle of France that is being staged. When the Exposition is over, the software would be dismantled and completely recycled. Certain display boxes can be dismantled and transferred along with their contents, to museums or partner organisations.

A scenario that is embedded in the theme of the Exposition and that structures the public's visit in thematic sequences composed of sets of display boxes is proposed. Finally, the programming of the most flexible media, such as the video or billboards, will be changing over the course of the Exposition.

Shanghai EXPO 2010 France Pavilion Competition

Project name: France Pavilion Proposal **Designer:** Rudy Ricciotti **Place in the competition:** Participation

Project Description:
The France Pavilion designed by Rudy Ricciotti for the World Exposition in Shanghai is a body in an environment both undefined and abundant.

Faced with multiple challenges, the proposal, inevitably functional, is intended to be accessible to a wide audience while emphasising know-how and "French excellence".

In line with the general theme of the Exposition "Better City, Better Life", the obviousness demands that logical urban, architectural and landscape plans are intrinsically linked to sustainable development. Spatial qualities and human scale relations in the long term are pursued.

If France can rely on the rich history of its land and its flavours, it must also demonstrate that with its base values. It is in a constant movement.

The urban project, aiming to create an atmosphere of a user friendly scale discarding any rudeness, suggests a pedestrian access from the south, thus freeing the ground space.

The site on the corner of the block with two distinctive facades, of which one is overlooking the river, suggests a building quite visible for its upper part.

The conception, playing on economising the site occupancy, is a strong message sent to visitors; the garden and its walkway developed around the building became the real introduction to the exhibition.

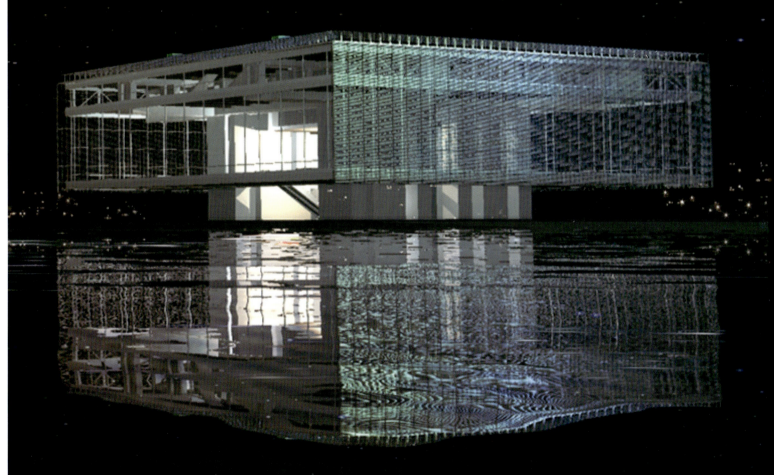

Shanghai EXPO 2010 France Pavilion Competition

Project name: France Pavilion Proposal — Elementary Pavilion **Designer:** Matthieu Poitevin & Pascal Reynaud **Place in the competition:** Participation

Project Description:

Essential and Elementary

Descartes' sky, whirls of ether at the origin of the movements of the planets, is the conceptual and physical matrix of this project. It links landscape and people. Ether is a spirit according to magicians. Here the pavilion is the elementary element and the fifth element, people is its spirit. The crowd shapes the building; the content holds the container. This pavilion is a human manifesto, for an emotional and effervescent architecture. It is rooted in the river, in Shanghai itself; it is a living, evolving landscape.

The Cave

Intimacy and reflection are at the core of this artistic development. By wandering in a sensory world, the designers try to script a new myth of contemporary artistic creation. France has been welcoming, mixing and making the most of various cultures from all horizons. This pavilion seeks after this process by making French and Chinese artists meet each other.

Descartes' Sky

The horizon of sensual dunes of Descartes becomes a garden. In fact, a garden is just a question of how to put a frame, of how to look at nature. Chinese gardens shape landscape through the emotions perceived.

The Cloud

Either suggesting sunshine or rain, the cloud makes the horizon effervescent. The tightrope walker and the acrobat turn its reality into a sensual show. Emotion rises from flesh and bones. But what is the Sixth Sense? Intuition or bliss.

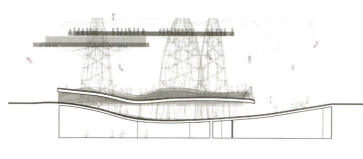

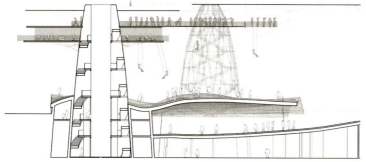

It is a sense sketch: an underground and sky.

Three steps for an ode to Time. The river symbolises Time, Travel, and a landmark on a road, on the road between France and Shanghai.

Sensation is no longer in Space, nor in Materiality. Sensation lies in Time, this is what the Fourth Dimension is!

Restructuring

What is the future of a building-to-be?

What is at stake with the pavilion is to say and show that style is content, that architecture and nature are linked, and they compensate each other ecologically.

Nowadays Shanghai is covering itself not only with buildings but also with great parks. Let's seek the ideal "Better City, Better Life" in this project. A different architecture rooted in soil, in nature, describes the landscape.

After the Exposition, it will be the same; only the uses of the building will have to be reinvented. Some potential is given to a pavilion, which becomes an elementary building…

Each of us needs to find his/ her own marks, to make his/her own choices. The France Pavilion is a free territory.

Shanghai EXPO 2010 France Pavilion Competition

Project name: France Pavilion Proposal — Cutting Up / Moving Up
Designer: Romain VIAULT / DESUNIQUES **Place in the competition:** Entry to the final

Project Description:

A large square will link the former factories rehabilitated into halls for the EXPO 2010 in Shanghai. It will help crossover a broad road. Located at the centre of the wide exhibition hall, the whole site is to federate. Besides, the location is divided along a broad road, while the former factories to rehabilitate are scattered. Seen as a puzzling game (cutting up / moving up), a large square will link the buildings, will enable the crossing over, and will shelter the shopping centre and the storage area. On the ground floor, areas on the two sides of the road are devoted to offices, restaurants, and entertainment. On the upper floor, exhibition halls are connected by a central square which, through the complex configuration of geometrical figures, gives a three dimensional sense. From the central square, one can have a good view of the road below. Meanwhile, a strip surrounding the square alternately gives way to urban furniture, lights and plants, contributing to the landscape of the whole site.

The exhibition halls are designed to be different from one another. According to specific needs, different functional areas are assigned to exhibition sections, including storage area, entrance area, business area, restaurant, and entertainment area. The halls are all composed with an entrance wrapped in a metal skin (in memory of the factored steel) to symbolise the exhibiting country. A set of roofs will enable natural light to penetrate into the heart of the large exhibition halls. In order to achieve a soft light effect, the designers tried many ways of natural lighting, using the existing slanting roof, and at the same time, created different shapes of the roof, adding

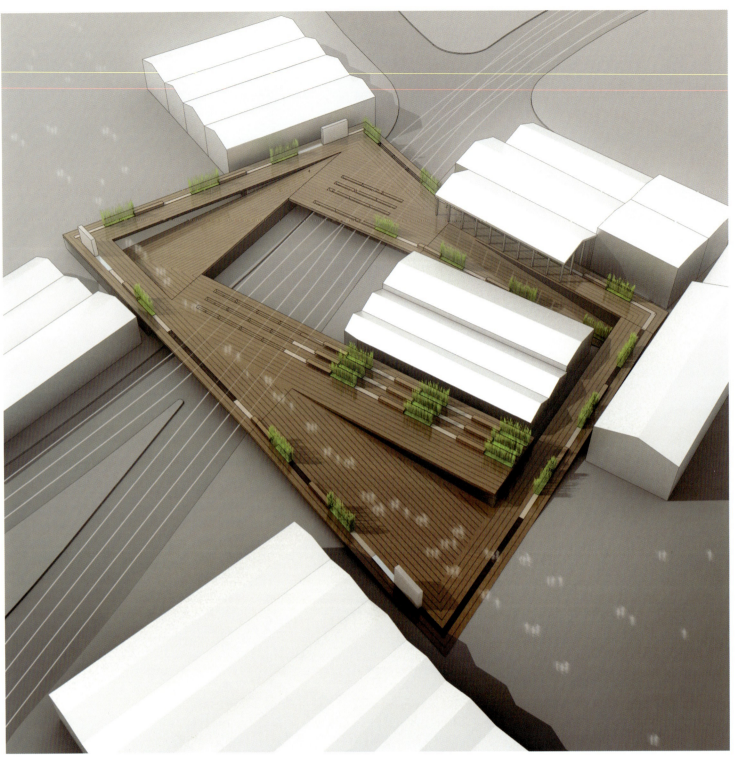

some aesthetic effects to the pavilion.

The design of the walls of the pavilion is quite eye-catching. The hollow-out of the surface, on the one hand, contributes to the exterior look of the pavilion; on the other hand, helps create a special shadowing effect for the interior.

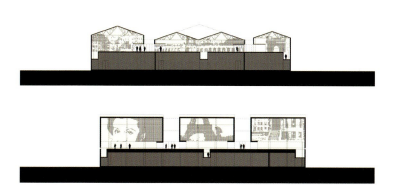

Shanghai EXPO 2010 Germany Pavilion Competition

Project name: German Pavilion — Balancity **Designer:** Schmidhuber + Kaindl GmbH, Munich (architecture + planning), Milla und Partner GmbH, Stuttgart (exhibition) **Place in the competition:** Winner **Organiser:** Koelnmesse International GmbH **Theme:** Harmonious City

Project Description:

The Germany Pavilion has been christened "balancity" – a newly coined word signifying a city in balance.

The journey starts at the harbour and leads through gardens and parks, via a town planning office and a factory and past a city square to end at the "Energy Source", the city's power plant, which is the heart of balancity and the highlight of the Germany Pavilion. It's an awe-inspiring, cone-shaped room with dramatic choreographed lighting. From a gallery, visitors can see the main attraction—a sphere, three metres in diameter and fitted with hundred thousands of LEDs. Pictures, colours and shapes appear on its surface, showing impulses from Germany for EXPO 2010. The sphere is set in motion, and the impulses triggered, by the audience, directed by Yanyan and Jens, the protagonists of balancity. Visitors can set the sphere swinging by making movements and shouting loudly. The sphere begins to swing back and forth. The further it swings, the more intensive the colours become. The sphere's energy is reflected throughout the room—on the balustrades, the walls, the ceiling and the floor.

The swinging initiated by the audience picks up speed and momentum and the sphere starts to move in a circular motion. Lots of different images of Germany and balancity race past the spectators' eyes. Then the sphere comes to a halt and there's silence. The room is bathed in green light and a pleasant, natural atmosphere sets in under a blue sky. From a globe, a seed grows, slowly turning into a flower—a symbol of new life.

The aim of the Germany Pavilion is to provide inspiration on how

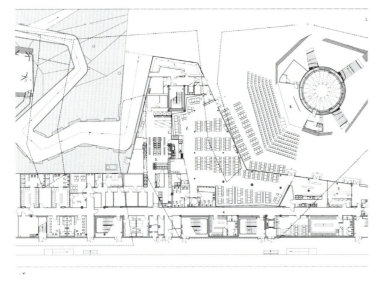

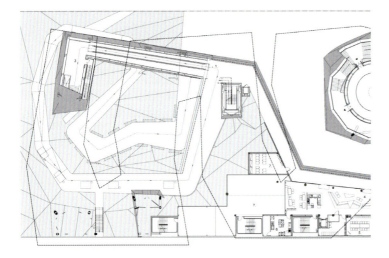

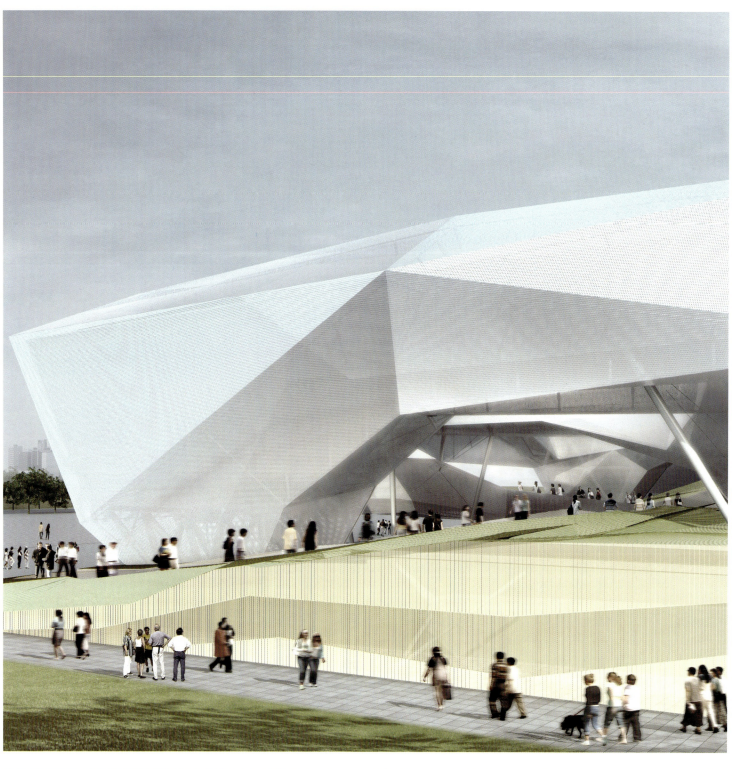

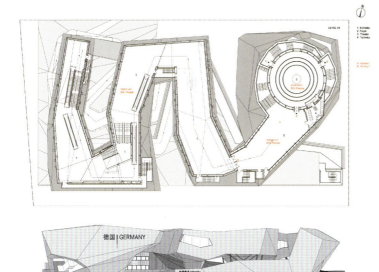

quality of life and diversity in cities can be enhanced by ensuring that the elements of which they are composed interact in harmony. The balance between renewal and preservation, community and individual development and globalisation and nationality is the core topic of the exhibition and is also reflected in the pavilion's architectural design.

Rather than being conceived as a building, the pavilion is meant to be a three dimensional walk-through sculpture with no defined interior or exterior. Instead, the EXPO Plaza (the square in front of the Germany Pavilion) and the surrounding landscape will simply flow into the pavilion.

The architecture will give the exhibition a "shell", facilitating it and giving it space to develop. The design takes its lead from the classic "promenade d'architecture".

Four large exhibition structures symbolise the interplay between the forces involved when loads are carried and applied, leant and supported.

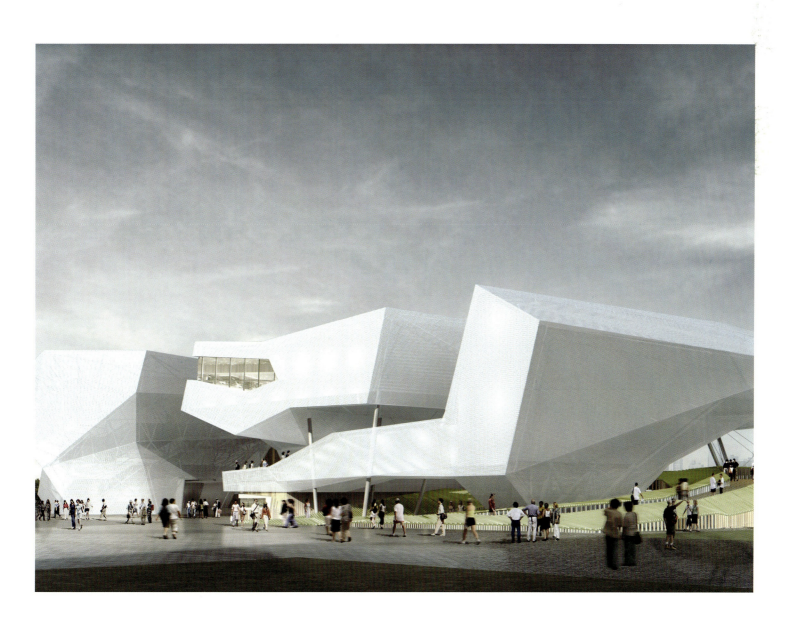

Project name: Hong Kong Pavilion—The Infinite City **Designer:** Joey Ho Design Ltd **Place in the competition:** Winner **Theme:** Hong Kong—The Infinite City and The Intellectual City

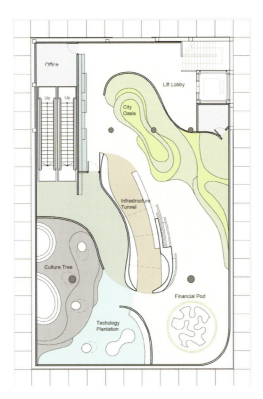

Shanghai EXPO 2010 Hong Kong Pavilion Competition

Project Description:

The design of the Hong Kong Pavilion for the 2010 Shanghai EXPO—The Infinite City, explains and explores the infinite possibilities and potentials that the city enjoys. Hong Kong is a place where the citizens share their dreams, overcome the crises and demonstrate their commitments to their families and their country. And most important of all, this is an ever-revitalising wonderland which promises us a brighter future.

A concept of "in-betweenness" advocated by Taoism has been incorporated into the programme of the pavilion, aiming to demonstrate the unique quality of Hong Kong, which allows her to develop and expand beyond its spatial and physical limitations. Inspired by the distinguished porosity nature of sponge, the design integrates the concept of "in-betweenness"—an infinite state that illustrates the unlimited possibilities and potentials of Hong Kong. Sponge is used as a metaphor; its tightly woven mass of spicules hang together very well and is enormously tough and this living tissue represents the united and never-give-up spirit of Hong Kong. The immense penetration capacity between the internal canals and cavities signifies the freedom, dynamism and openness of this cosmopolitan city.

The pavilion takes the form of a cube structure in double layers with the outer layer converted into a series of bamboo section modules. Special lightings are deployed to give the golden cube a glowing effect. At night it is transformed into a lantern reminiscent of an exquisite jewel box. The reflective pool and mirror covered around the lift core give a sense of lightness to the

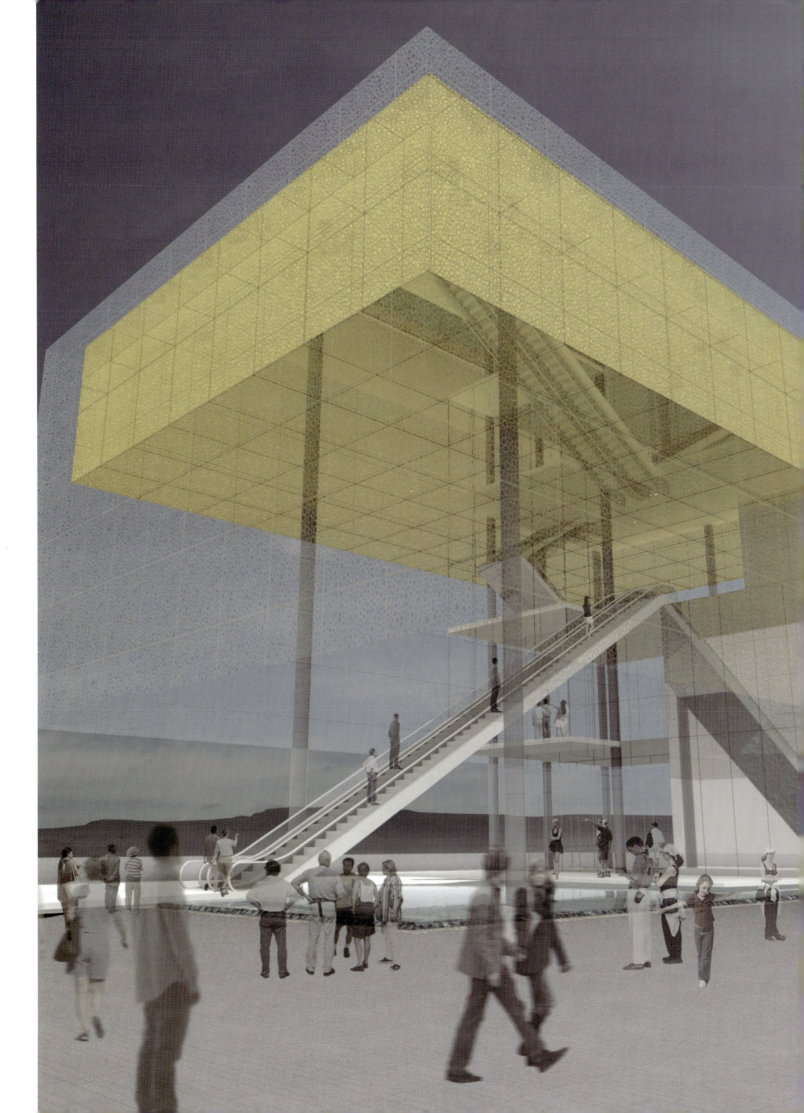

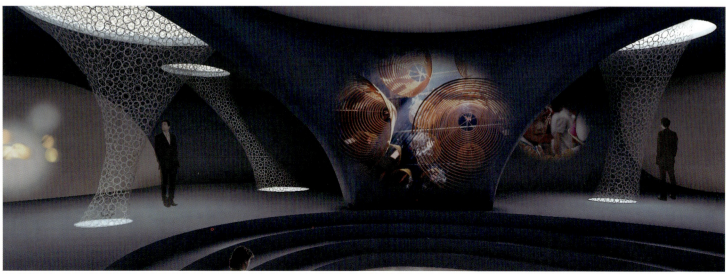

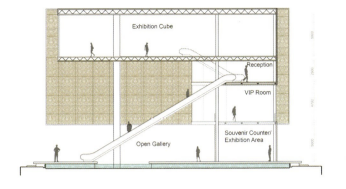

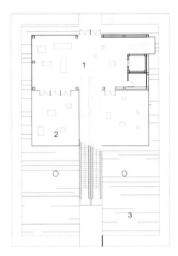

building.

The external façade of the pavilion is built by square modules made up of bamboo sections. This environmentally friendly material, when cut into sections, allows sunlight and breeze to penetrate into the building. In addition to the advantage of energy saving, the bamboo modules can also be easily disassembled and recycled for other use. Combined with the water feature and modern courtyard design that open up the ground level for communal use and natural cooling, the pavilion presents a simple yet cost-effective green building concept.

While the pavilion's outlook appears to be relatively restrained and calm, the interior surprises visitors with a stunning impact through various interactive and vibrant design approaches. Following the same building tissue that echoes with the external bamboo façade, each of the five zones - Culture Tree, Technology Plantation, Infrastructure Tunnel, Financial Pod and City Oasis - carries its own uniqueness. The fluidity and dynamic tension of space enrich the sensational experience.

Shanghai EXPO 2010 Hungary Pavilion Competition

Project name : Hungary Pavilion **Designer:** Tamás Lévai **Place in the competition:** Winner **Organiser:** Special Envoy of Prime Minister

Project Description:

Gömböc, as a Hungarian invention, is the central element of the exhibition, a two metre high solid plexiglass moving object. "Gömböc" is the first known homogenous object with one stable and one unstable equilibrium point, thus with two equilibria altogether on a horizontal surface. It can be proven that no object with less than two equilibria exists.

The discovery of the inaccessible path has led to the idea of Gömböc. The pavilion made of wood is intended to represent this path, and since it is of immaterial nature, the designers are trying to evoke it with non materials: empty space, light and sounds. Gömböc, as a distinguished pebble analogy, helps to understand empty space and to recognise its uniqueness and greatness. In order to represent it in architecture, the designers had to combine features that are shared by both mathematics and architecture: homogeneity, abstraction, dynamics and playfulness. The buffer space behaves as a wood opening, created from a three dimensional matrix of vertically moving wooden, sound tubes. The wooden installation in itself is like a musical instrument; the tubes are sound-boxes.

The appearing elements in the exhibition space constitute a harmonious unity in them, embodying the phenomenon that is created through the structure. It raises the opportunity of open-air exhibition with the moving light-sound-space, as a synthesis of nature.

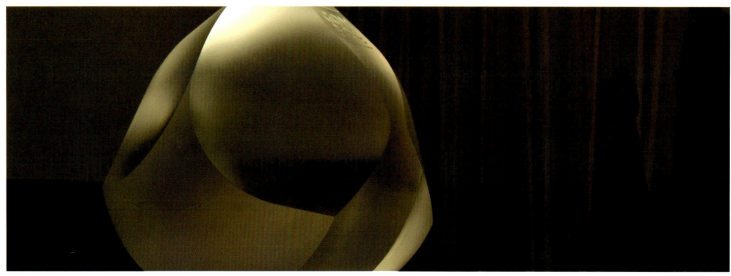

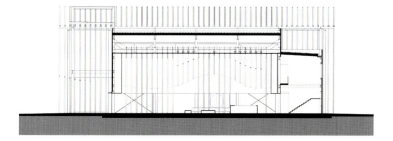

Shanghai EXPO 2010 Hungary Pavilion Competition

Project name: Hungary Pavilion Proposal — Gömböc **Designer:** Mérték Architectural Studio, Paulinyi Gergely (Head of Atelier) **Architects:** Bodola Péter Archibald, Fülöp Alex, Lukács Zsombor, Szirmai Balázs **Place in the competition:** Competition entry

Project Description:

Hungarian inscription has been defined and secured with the conception of attendance, according to a single and extremely simple 21st century invention, the "Gömböc" (meaning "globe" in Hungarian) that must be drawn around the Hungarian attendance; that is to say the "Gömböc" as an object and a thought plays the main role in the Hungarian Pavilion.

"Gömböc" is the first homogeneous object, which has one stable and one unstable point; that is to say, altogether there are two trim spots. While this is a mathematical breakthrough, the detected "Gömböc" can be easily transferred to such a strong symbolic world as the oriental cultures dispose. These two things, the interconnection of the Hungarian scientific breakthrough and the oriental culture, typify as a kinetic statue at the central axis of the pavilion, which demonstrates the "Gömböc" in the most expressive position for the duration of movement.

In retrospect, knowledge has been the most important and world standard EXPOrts in the history of Hungary. Incredible scientists, searchers, and professionals have existed to be able to effectively service millions of people. The authoritative theme of the exhibition provides facility to be able to represent these achievements in the world's scientific life by means of its collection. "Gömböc", as the symbol of balance, organically attaches to not only the chain of the historical achievements, but the thought of the maintainable growth as well, which is the principle of "Better City, Better Life". The design goal is the appearance of a positive and creative knowledge; significantly expands the value of universal humanity, a

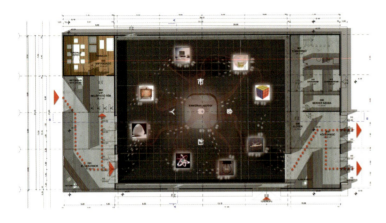

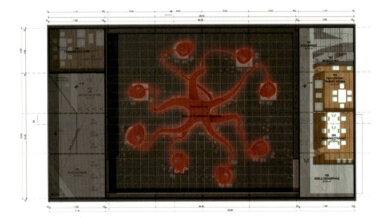

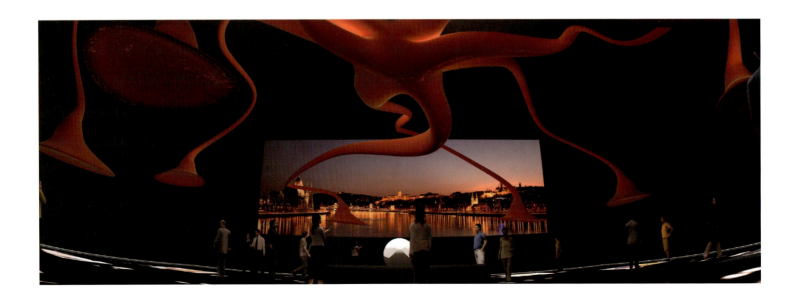

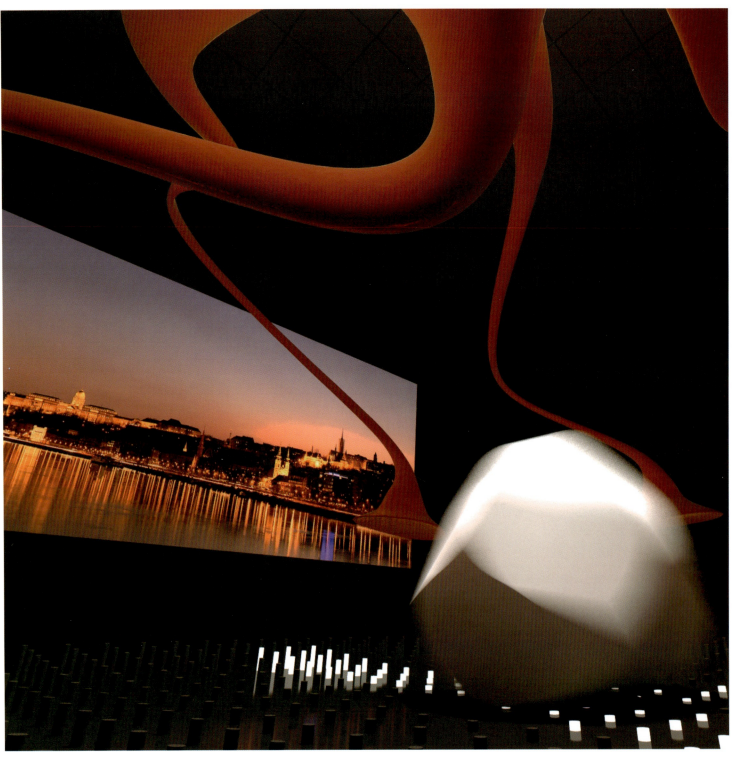

dynamically alternate country image for visitors.

The Hungary Pavilion appears as a consignment of an extraneous culture in the environment of Shanghai. Its clean form, reference of carton architectural components, as well as the adaptation of international signal system, have been desired to represent the character of the package.

At the exhibition, significant aspects have been the moderate and underlying characteristics to enhance the uniqueness of the exhibition's objects, synchronising with the underlying principles of the present museum architecture. The different functions of the pavilion can be convenient with changeable lighting and equipment system. Inside, the hanging graphic arts, as the symbol of knowledge and the form of brain have been suggested. The amorphous form, eight scientific themes that indicate Hungarian achievements, appears with recessed LCD monitors on floor.

On the whole, the design goal of plan, with architectural tools and the formation of space, prove a country image of an advanced and opened collaboration towards the hosts, which subsists two different cultures as an opportunity, instead of a barrage.

Shanghai EXPO 2010 Hungary Pavilion Competition

Project name: Hungary Pavilion Proposal — Gömböc Shell **Designer:** Urban Landscape Group: Principle architects: Barbara Szöllőssy: Zsolt Pkya; **Project designer:** Judit Z. Halmágyi,Zita Balajti **Place in the competition:** Competition entry

Project Description:

Gömböc conveys two messages: on the one hand it expresses that the Hungarians since centuries, driven by some energy, have recovered on their own from the most dangerous and severe situations; on the other hand, it represents China's resoluteness to revive and reconstruct its society. It is a new approach based on human values which contains values, articulated throughout the whole world and gathers its strength from Chinese overall philosophy. Such values are: liveability, environmental consciousness and sustainable development. Their conception along with their philosophy is based on knowledge. Here meets the idea of the discovery of Gömböc, constantly renewing re-interpretation and balance-making.

The pavilion's basic idea is Gömböc, balance-searching of a homogeneous material in our space of gravity. The pavilion by unfolding Gömböc's surface into shells continues mathematic and shell-calculation experiments of inventors with a declared purpose to unfold shell pieces in multiple layers similar to Chinese luck ball, thus creating a smaller aura, an open but exciting and abstract space from the endless space. The pavilion's exterior is a transformed and dissected Gömböc, by opening which we can visualise its theory.

The shells seemingly refer to lines of Chinese Emperors Palace, placed on artificial stone and light-transmitting concrete platform. Gömböc, as described by its inventor a "spatial Yin Yang" according to Chinese Feng Shui philosophy, is here in a building; still, it has the same impression as it would be outside in nature.

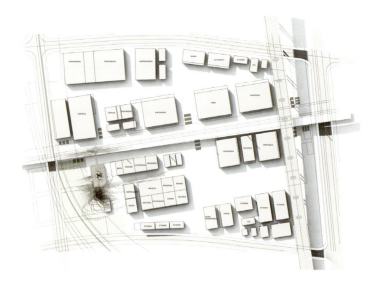

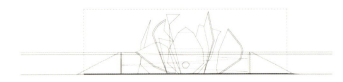

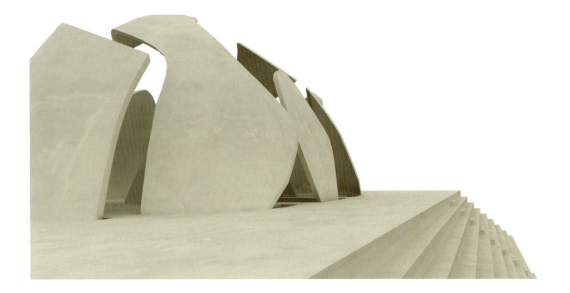

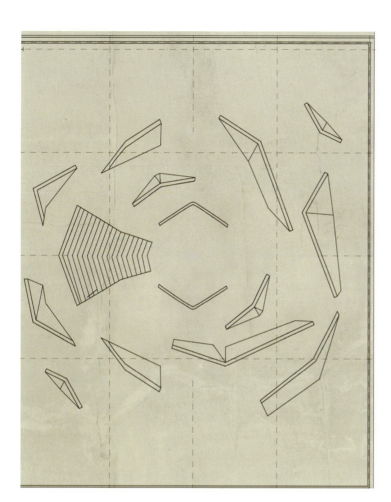

Thus, the designers wished to express the presence of cosmic energy in spaces created with lyrical shapes and forms.

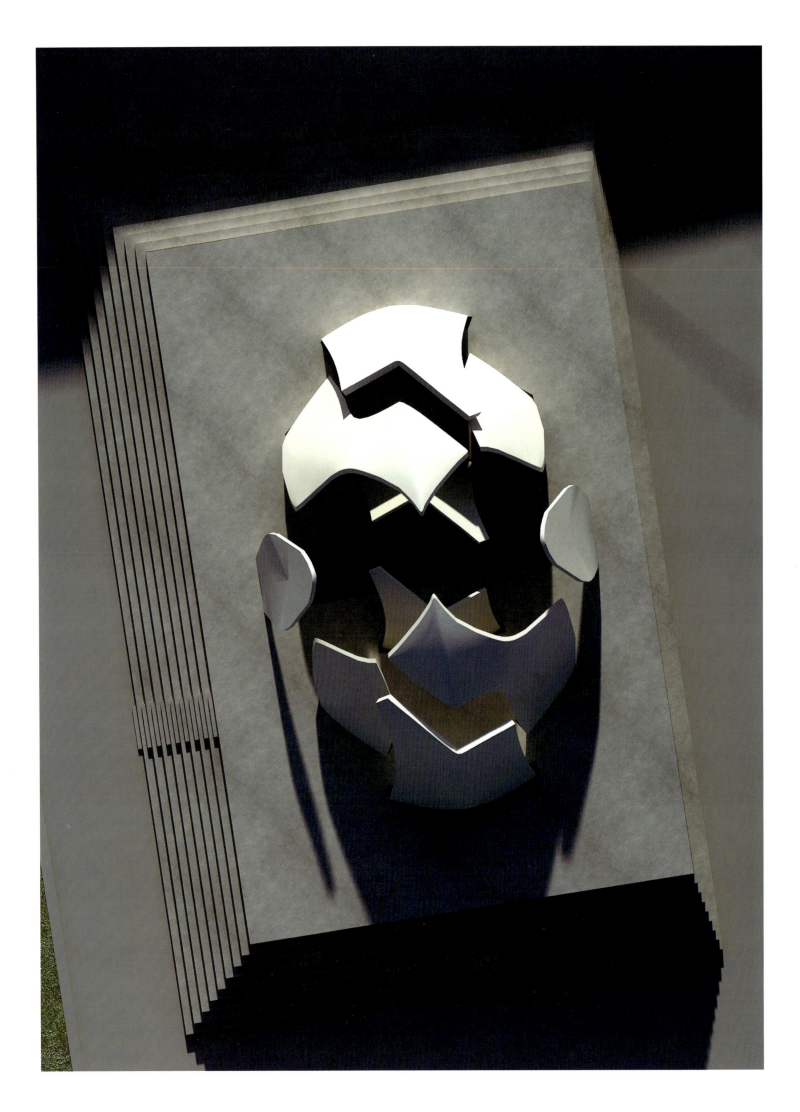

Shanghai EXPO 2010 Iceland Pavilion Competition

Project name: Iceland Pavilion **Designer:** Pall Hjaltason, +ARKITEKTAR; Arnbjorg Haflidadottir, Saga-Events **Place in the competition:** Winner **Organiser:** Iceland Ministry for Foreign Affairs **Theme:** Pure Energy, Healthy Living

Project Description:

This Iceland Pavilion project was judged for its innovative character, its functionality, as well as its unity and compatibility with the spatial requirements of the Exposition's organiser. The assessment took into consideration the concept of the Exposition's programme, the cost of the project and its execution.

The project is a simple design and a memorable concept that is closely connected to the image of Iceland. This project not only fulfils the expectations of the country and the responsibility for presenting its achievements and successes, but also brings Chinese visitors closer to Iceland. It will enable those visitors who are not familiar with Iceland to receive a favourable image of the country through exciting presentations.

The official theme of Iceland's participation in EXPO 2010 in Shanghai is "Pure Energy, Healthy Living", reflecting how Icelanders have developed a friendly relationship with natural forces and learned how to harvest its energy to improve their life. Iceland is home to one of the world's most active networks of volcanoes, geysers, rivers and glaciers. Together they create an abundant resource for non-polluting energy production, both hydro and geothermal. Over 99% of Icelandic power consumption comes from renewable sources, with minimal exhaust pollution. Iceland's unique nature thus remains pristine and largely un-touched to this day and Iceland's capital city, towns and villages remain clean and green.

The Icelandic people live longer and healthier lives as a consequence of their pure energy and clean environment. The

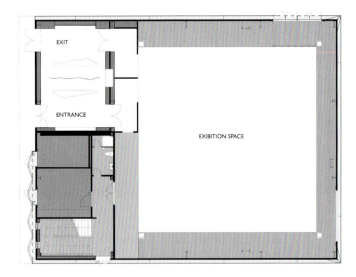

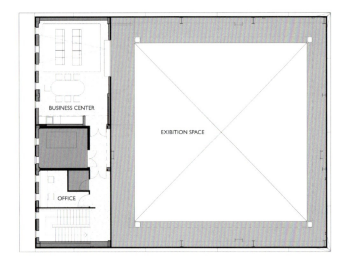

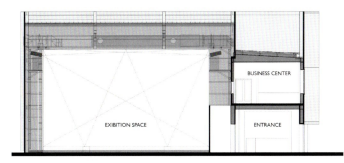

local economy depends on large fishing grounds in the Northern Atlantic as its primary product while a diversified service sector has developed to include state of the art hospitals, universities of advanced learning and some of the world's most progressive and successful firms in their field, particularly within food industry, prosthetics and gaming. Iceland's people and industry reap the benefits of cheap green energy, which coupled with its educated labour force, highly developed infrastructure and strategic location between Europe and North America, making Iceland a destination of choice for geographically strategic foreign direct investment. Reykjavik, Iceland's capital is home to half the country's population. It is a modern, vibrant and prosperous city that combines green spaces, traditional wooden houses with their typical colourful roofs and an efficient transport system. Icelandic urbanites are health conscious and ambitious. Their creativity forms the basis for Iceland's vibrant cultural life that includes performers such as Björk and Sigur Rós, whose international recognition has grown to greater proportions than one might anticipate from such a proportionally small country.

The Iceland EXPO Pavilion seeks to explain the fundamental relationship between nature and energy on the one hand, and Iceland's people, urban areas and culture on the other. With an encompassing high definition video projection, a story of survival and success unfolds, bringing visitors to the Shanghai EXPO to the peaceful and crystal clean environment of Iceland.

Project name: Ireland Pavilion **Designer:** Office of Public Works

Shanghai EXPO 2010 Ireland Pavilion

Project Description:

The Ireland Pavilion is a modern expression of urban design. Sharply defined and finished in natural cool tones, it rises behind landforms evocative of Ireland's coastal setting. The pavilion has five enclosed galleries, amounting to over 1,500 square metres of exhibition space, arranged on a series of levels. Gently inclined slopes permit progress through all the galleries in sequence.

The exhibition galleries are arranged in rectangular form around a courtyard plaza that will be both an exhibition space and a performance area for many of the presentations in the promotional and cultural programme being developed for EXPO 2010.

On entering the Ireland Pavilion, the initial exhibit will establish for all visitors the geography and identity of Ireland. Visitors will proceed along a gently ramped long gallery through a presentation of the character of urban living in Ireland through the ages. The visitor arrives into the elevated first gallery in which the essential character of Irish cityscape is presented with the architecture of ages as the background, giving a vivid impression of contemporary Irish cities. Audio visual presentations will provide direct viewing links and allow Irish cities to be observed in real time.

A VIP Lounge is located at the highest level and opens onto the landscaped roofs. Ancillary and office spaces are located beneath the ramped spaces at plinth level.

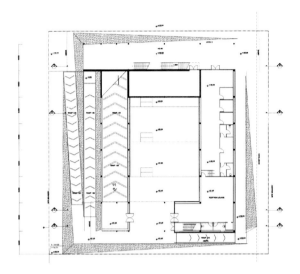

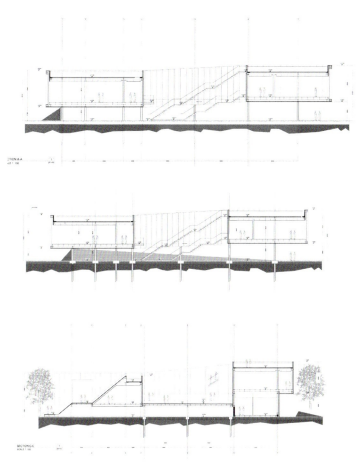

Shanghai EXPO 2010 Israel Pavilion Competition

Project name: Israel Pavilion **Designer:** Haim Dotan **Place in the competition:** Winner **Theme:** Better Innovation, Better Life

Project Description:

The national Israel Pavilion for the World EXPO 2010 in Shanghai is an innovative and futuristic architectural structure symbolising breakthrough and technology. The 1,200 square metres pavilion is built on a 2,000 square metres site.

The pavilion is composed of two architectural curvilinear forms which hug each other like two hands or two shells. The two dynamic forms symbolise a quiet conversation between man and earth, man and man, nation and nation. They represent the dialogue between man and nature, past and future, temporality and eternity, earth and sky, substance and virtual. Within the two forms are two uplifting architectural spaces, symbolising the spirituality of the ancient Jewish nation.

The project consists of three experiential realms: Whispering Garden, Hall of Light and Hall of Innovations.

Whispering Garden:

Located between a plaza and the Israel Pavilion, the Whispering Garden symbolises the dialogue between man and nature. The inviting garden serves as a pleasant green orchard where 300 Chinese visitors wait in queue before entering the building. Walking on a covered path between whispering trees, visitors are protected from heat of the sun and the rain and may rest on available benches.

Hall of Light:

Entering the pavilion, visitors are uplifted by a dynamic, high architectural space symbolising the dialogue between man and man. Enclosed in clear glass, the space is illuminated by natural

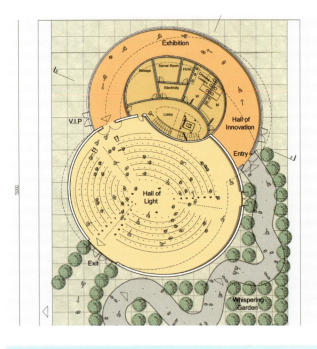

daylight and is an expression of future, optimism and breakthrough. While walking along a curved wall, visitors experience an exhibition of Jewish historical innovations from Biblical times forward. During the day and night, millions of Chinese visitors strolling on the adjacent pedestrian bridge outside the Israel Pavilion view displays of technological innovations projected on the 15-metre high wall inside the glass space of the pavilion. Thus a dialogue is created between the outside and the inside, enticing the public. Located within the curved pavilion wall are a VIP and employee lobby, stairs, an elevator to the upper floor, changing rooms, and storage and mechanical rooms. On the upper floor are management and secretariat offices, an employee dining room and a VIP lounge for cultural and business gatherings.

Hall of Innovations:

As a lofty space of 20 metres in height, accommodating 300 visitors, the Hall of Innovations is the climax of the Israel Pavilion. It creates an uplifting feeling of amazement and excitement for visitors. First, interactive light balls in front of spectators transmit messages from Israeli children and adults in Hebrew and Chinese to Chinese spectators.

Then, an audio-visual show of light balls floating in the dynamic space is projected on a 360-degree display, revealing new worlds of Israeli innovations and technological breakthroughs in the fields of archaeology, agriculture and irrigation, botany and food, medicine, solar and green energy, sciences, music, literature and many fields of hi-tech, and communications and security.

Shanghai EXPO 2010 Israel Pavilion Competition

Project name: Israel Pavilion Proposal **Designer:** Knafo Klimor Architects
Place in the competition: Entry to the final

Project Description:

The design motive of the Israel Pavilion is a structure in the form of a book – a book representing the source of knowledge, culture, language and heritage. The book, as a wellspring of ideas, narratives, facts and fictions, safeguards the historic memory and cultural background of a community and its people.

The main body of the exhibition is planned along a route spanning three floors:

The mezzanine shows multimedia screen projections on medicine, high-tech, communication, aerospace, agriculture and tourism.

The upper floor, exposed to direct sunlight, houses an ecological garden, presenting the ecological challenges Israel is currently facing – effectively harnessing solar energy, water treatment and re-use, soil fertility and problems abounding in deserts and arid regions.

The ground level includes a 300-seat auditorium for cultural events included in the pavilion programme.

The Israel Pavilion plan revolves around the principles of green architecture, in terms of both the building's enveloping structure and its interior. The structure consists of double-layered plastic sleeves and plates encasing a steel construction. The casing is made of recyclable, environmentally-friendly materials that can be reused in the future. The spacing between walls is fed with cool air intended to insulate the surface and ventilate the pavilion interior,

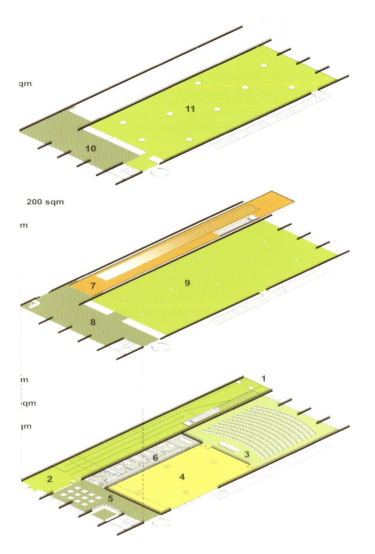

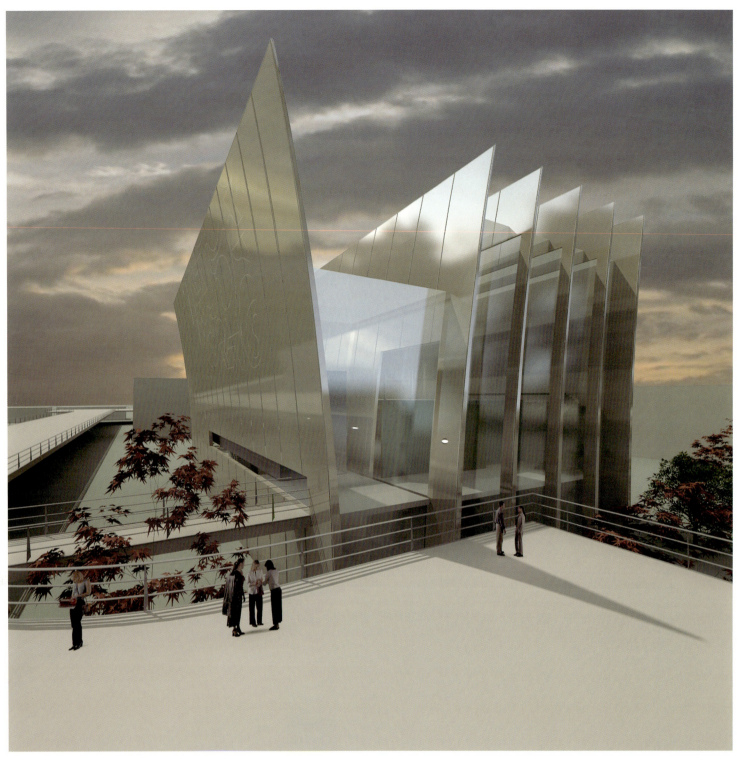

thus presenting an advanced technological solution while reducing maintenance costs.

Shanghai EXPO 2010 Italy Pavilion Competition

Project name: Italy Pavilion **Designer:** Giampaolo Imbrighi **Organiser:** Commission of Italy World EXPO 2010 Shanghai **Theme:** A City of Ideal, A City of People

Project Description:
Design Concept
The project proposes a building which integrates a typical model of Italian urban building, with the architectural structure of the Chinese construction game called Shanghai.

Distribution Characteristics:
The pavilion covers an area of 3,600 square metres and is 18 metres high. Inside, the pavilion is divided into irregular sections of different dimensions, connected by a steel bridge structure where the connecting galleries are visible. If needed, the structure can be dismantled and reconstructed, on a smaller scale, in another part of the city.

Architectonic Characteristics:
The different sections of the building make up a geometrical variety symbolising the tradition and regional customs which define the Italian identity: a type of mosaic of which each of the parts show a single picture. The form also highlights the topographic complexity of Italian cities, with numerous short narrow roads and alleys which suddenly open onto a large square, a characteristic which can also be found in traditional Chinese urban centres. A psychophysical effect of comfort is given by an internal garden, the presence of water and natural light which spreads throughout the area across the patios and by the walls.

New Material:
The building is decorated on three sides by a film of water that reflects the structure, highlighting the natural shiny effects. The brilliance of the structure, reproduced inside both via slits evokes

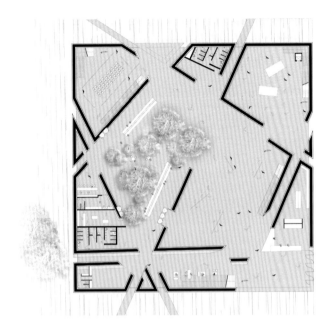

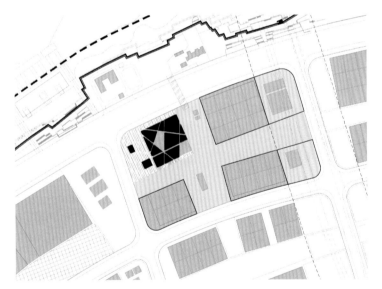

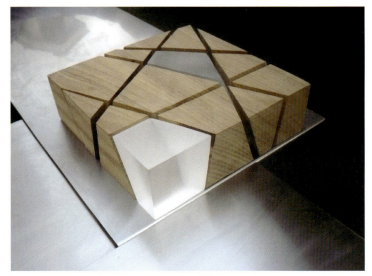

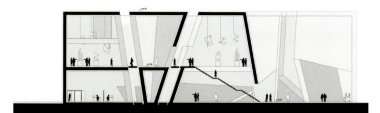

the narrow alleys between the city buildings, and also thanks to the use of transparent cement, a new, recently created multifaceted material. Because of its particular and diverse components on different sides of the building, this material generates a twofold architectural effect: from the outside a nocturnal effect of the liveliness inside, and from the inside, the outside daylight atmosphere. The surface of the pavilion will appear transparent with the sides made up of self-cleaning glass.

Bioclimatic Function:

The pavilion has been created as if it were a bioclimatic "machine" with the aim of saving energy. The photovoltaic elements integrated in the glass covering guarantee protection from radiation, while the light-technologies of the building not only aims at highlighting the spaces, but also favours the saving of energy.

Shanghai EXPO 2010 Italy Pavilion Competition

Project name: Italy Pavilion Proposal **Designer:** BiCuadro Architects
Francesco Bezzi Massimiliano Brugia Valerio Campi **Collaborator:** Stefano
Farcomeni Architect **Place in the competition:** Entry to the final

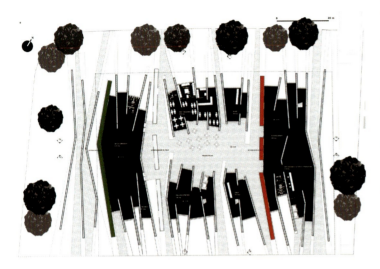

Project Description:

"Better City for Better Life". The project presents the Italian style through a design inspired by the authentic expression of the Italian city: "the historical stratified city".

While big metropolises of the 21st century are having a crisis of sustainability because of wrong growth and environmental alienation, the Italian urban system, which is based on continuity with the historical and the geographical background, is still working well and produces high quality lifestyle.

"The Italian stratified city" keeps resisting the modern processes of alienation of inhabitants. It also represents a strong human spatial entity that can be perceived psychologically by people. It is connected to the past. Its tissue was built up during centuries and through several generations so that life of its inhabitants is strictly related to it.

The Italia Piazza is the centre of this entity. It is the core that cannot be replaced. It is the place of "being" and "staying", a very important case study, where Art is also expressed. It is a unique "spatial circumstance".

The Italy Pavilion for Shanghai is the representation of this "spatial circumstance" which also produces and gives birth to excellence. It is a prototype that expresses the stratification of the social and urban Italian soul and gives the idea of historical continuity.

The guide line of the project is a volume divided into several planes, representing a timeline as a metaphor of the rise of the Italian urban tissue.

20 planes, as many as the Italian departments, are separated by

three window planes where the Made in Italy products are shown. They are the main structure of the pavilion on the floor plan.
The interior Exposition spaces are influenced by this spatial scan and are organised between the planes as different theme streams. Walking inside the building is like strolling through history.
The building grows around a plaza. Visitors discover this plaza just by walking in as the planes hide it from the exterior. This gives the same feeling as you would get by exploring an old Italian city or town.

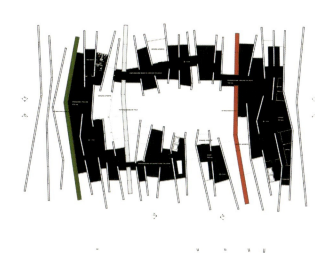

made in italy

Shanghai EXPO 2010 Italy Pavilion Competition

Project name: Italy Pavilion Proposal **Proposal Designer:** Manfredi Nicoletti **Place in the competition:** Participation

Project Description:

The pavilion's dynamic shape represents Italian innovation and fantasy, meanwhile the "Better City, Better Life" theme is represented through the main features of Italian urban quality. The pavilion's structure, raised up from the ground, is the metaphor of a flying bird. The surface is shaped in accord with a warped geometry, the same as many living creatures such as leaves and animals.

The pavilion is suspended upon a white platform surrounded by water pools, and represents some specific Italian qualities: lightness, agility, elegance and soaring.

The steel structure grants the precision of a prefabricated assembling system which, as a result, will have an easy and economic construction. Three columns with stairs and services are going to support a horizontal structure with suspended floors. There will be no other structural parts, in order to obtain an internal space entirely opened and free.

Under the pavilion a space similar to the Italian square is provided, protected by the sun, refreshed by water, and opened to the surroundings. Here, a circular island will host different kinds of shows.

Inside the pavilion nature and city are integrated as it uniquely happens in Italian cities. The first floor is covered with a grass surface and the three columns are representative of city buildings.

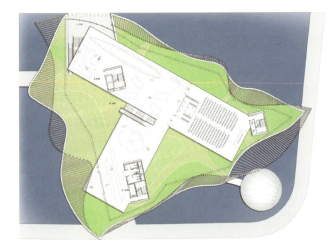

Shanghai EXPO 2010 Korea Pavilion Competition

Project name: Korea Pavilion **Designer:** Mass **Place in the competition:** Winner **Organiser:** KOTRA - Korea Trade-Investment Promotion Agency **Theme:** Friendly City, Colourful Life

Project Description:

With a "land culture" (China) and a "sea culture" (Japan) surrounding the peninsula, Korea has been permeable to exotic cultures and global influences, whose progressive mix defines contemporary Korean society. Using "convergence" as the main theme, the Korea Pavilion is an amalgamation of "sign" (symbol) and "space": Signs become spaces, and simultaneously, spaces become signs.

Han-geul, the Korean alphabet, is the prime element of "signs" within the pavilion. The overall volume, lifted 7.2 metres above ground level, is created by converging these Han-geul letters, allowing signs to create the exhibition space, and so that visitors can experience their geometry through horizontal, vertical and diagonal movements. The primary geometries that compose the Han-geul letters are universal to other cultures, thus acting as an inviting set of signs that is engaging to everyone.

The exterior surfaces of the Korea Pavilion are clad in two types of pixels: Han-geul Pixels and Art Pixels. Han-geul Pixels are white panels with a relief of letters in four different sizes whose combination forms the majority of the exterior, mainly the peripheral surfaces. Most of the non-peripheral surfaces are composed of Art Pixels, which are 45 centimetres by 45 centimetres aluminium panels created by a Korean artist, Ik-Joong Kang. About 40,000 of these panels will texture the façade, contributing a bright palette of colours, hope, and unity throughout the Korea Pavilion. The surfaces will project different atmospheres during the day and night, with light and shadows creating different textures. Sequential

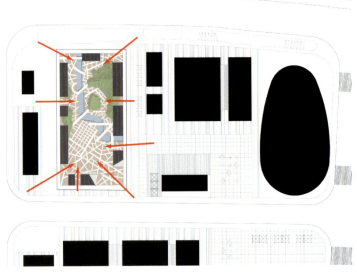

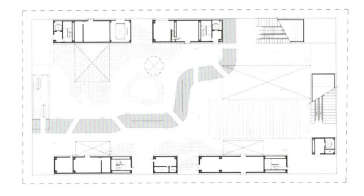

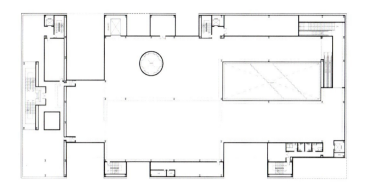

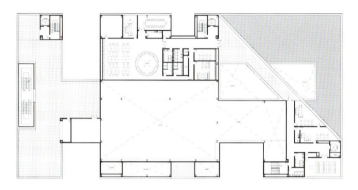

lighting is installed behind the Han-geul Pixels to highlight the individual letters on the exterior façade at night, further animating the pavilion as a sign (like a text message) on a larger scale. By the understanding of a map as a sign that depicts space, the designers have translated the ground level piloti space as a sign, by making an abstract 1/300 scale 3D map of a characteristic Korean city as its surface. The rest of the building, containing the exhibition space, is suspended seven metres above to create a 40 metres by 77 metres free, open space generated by the map. The map becomes a semi-exterior landscape that expresses the converging of mountains, water, and a dense metropolitan area, as exemplified by Seoul, the national capital. This ground floor is shaded by the main volume and additionally cooled by the replica of a river (modelled after the Han River) flowing from one corner to the other as a five metres wide, 79 metres long artificial stream, while the notable mountains become stages/seating/spaces for visitors to enjoy shows while queued in line to enter the exhibition space above. There is also a series of LED monitors, a large LED screen and two water screen projections to assist the interaction with visitors.

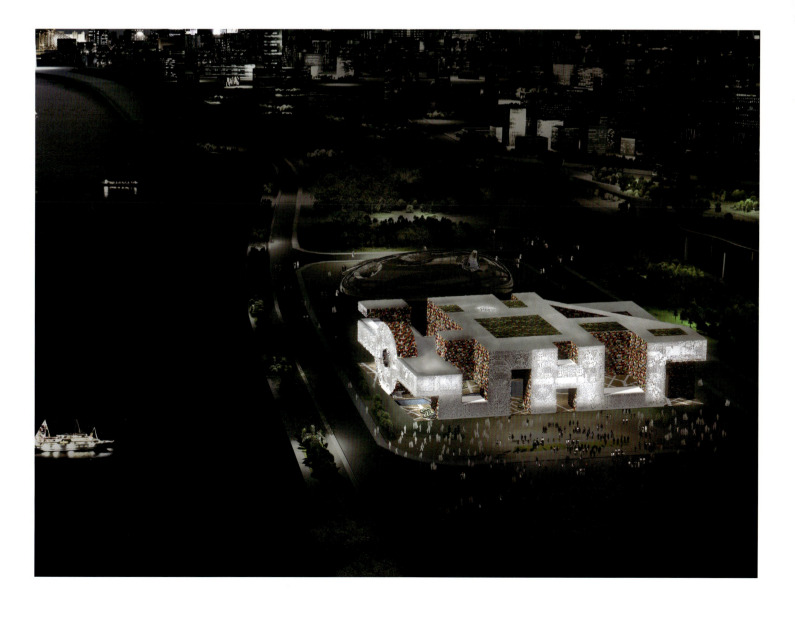

Project name: Luxembourg Pavilion **Designer:** Hermann & Valentiny and Associates **Place in the competition:** Winner **Organiser:** Shanghai EXPO **Theme:** Small is Beautiful Too

Shanghai EXPO 2010 Luxembourg Pavilion Competition

Project Description:

Luxembourg is small. Because of that fact, it often passes unnoticed. Some people have never heard of it, especially outside continental Europe. While six million Chinese tourists visited France in 2006, only 100,000 found their way to Luxembourg. The Shanghai World EXPO exhibition is therefore an occasion for Luxembourg to boost its profile on the Asian continent. Shanghai is one of the world's largest, most modern and fastest-developing cities. So it is difficult to impress the Chinese with Luxembourg's technology and architecture. Though the Luxemburgues define their country as small, they could attract visitors' attention by revealing the secrets of their prosperity to the world as their characteristic flexibility, neutrality, openness, integration of foreigners and mediation.

Pavilion visitors will be able to find out many advantages of living in a small country. One of the most welcome is that this is a peaceful country, a country on a human scale. Here authorities and leaders are close to their people: a rarity.

In Chinese, "Luxembourg" means forest and fortress ("lúsēn bǎo"). That is why the Luxembourg Pavilion, designed in steel to represent the country's architecture, nevertheless incorporates green spaces. By modifying the scale and transforming the shape of traditional Luxembourg houses, the designers have sought to maximise symbiosis between the architectures of China and

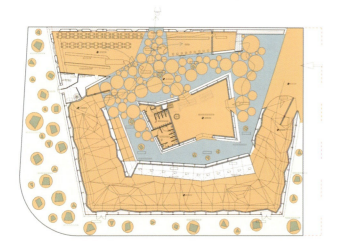

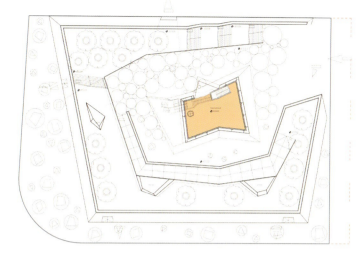

Luxembourg. They have studied functions and movement patterns on the theme of "lúsēn bǎo," linking them with Chinese Feng-Shui philosophy.

Basically, the design consists of two major parts, the enclosure and the tower in the courtyard of the enclosure. The main visitor areas are located in the enclosure, including the main exhibition space and a restaurant. Technical facility rooms are located in the enclosure as well. The central tower includes at the level of +0.00 metre a multifunctional auditorium and WC facilities for visitors and the staff. It includes at the level of +2.82 metres two office rooms for the staff of the pavilion. At the level of +9.01 metres a special VIP floor is located. This VIP floor will only be accessible after prior approval or invitation of the building owner. This floor includes a fold-out balcony which can be opened for special occasions and venues.

The roof of the enclosure is accessible for visitors as well. The height of the roof of the enclosure diversifies between +5.04 metres (in the northern part) and +5.46 metres. The balustrade has a current height of +6.13 metres. The height of the tower in its highest point is +21.35 metres and is verified and proofed by the technical office of the World EXPO. The carrying structure of the project is made of steel I-sections. The foundation will be made of steel piles. The cladding of the main structure framework will be made by Cor-Ten steel panels of a thickness of four millimetres for the two buildings,the enclosure and the tower. The interior will be covered by timber panels according to the European "Brettstapelbau". The sections of the wooden scantlings will be 200 millimetres by 50 millimetres and 250 millimetres by 50 millimetres. The length of the scantlings will vary according to the architectural deign.

Project name: Luxembourg Pavilion Proposal   **Designer:** Marc Schmit
Place in the competition: Entry to the final

Shanghai EXPO 2010 Luxembourg Pavilion Competition

Project Description:

The aim of the project was to create an image that describes Luxembourg as a participant in the contemporary discourse of the city of the future.

The tightly woven global networks on a cultural and economic level will induce that the actual site doesn't necessarily play an important role any more. Simultaneously the pressure on urban centres is increasing. The pavilion consists of an individual volume. The selected nodes of the network represent Luxembourg. The various volumes are interwoven like foam bubbles.

The pavilion can be set up with inflatable walls and spaces depending on the programmes. It adapts itself flexibly to the needs of the exhibition. Digital presentation techniques make it possible to have individual and changing content. Thus the skin of the pavilion will change its appearances depending on different events.

The pavilion consist of a supporting structure steel structure. The primary system is steel rings that intersect at minimum three points, thus providing stiffness. After the positioning of the steel framework, ETFE cushions are mounted and inflated (e.g. Allianz Arena Munich, Eden Project Cornwall). Unlike in an air house (e.g. inflatable tennis halls), not the entire space is under pressure but only a layer of air inside the ETFE cushions. This works as an insulation layer. With the installation of this material and the constructing system, the pavilion is fully recyclable.

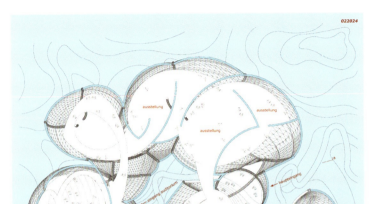

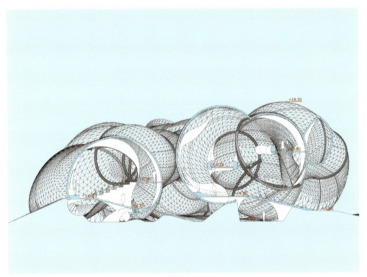

Shanghai EXPO 2010 Macau Pavilion Competition

Project name: Macau Pavilion **Desinger:** Carlos Marreiros **Place in the competition:** Winner **Organiser:** Office for Preparation of Macau's Participation in the Shanghai World EXPO of the Macao SAR

Project Description:

Who doesn't remember the Little Rabbit Lanterns, with a candle inside, trolling through the traditional streets of Macau, on a leash held by children, both Chinese and Portuguese, during the popular Moon Cake Festival?

These traditional Chinese lanterns were made by local skilful craftsmen, who fitted, a simple and light structure, with thin strips of bamboo or twig, which was covered with some layers of translucent and multicoloured paper, or with a layer of cellophane paper, and topped with ornaments of golden and silver paper, or simple paintings. However, during the last two decades, with the appearance of plastic "traditional lanterns" with lights fed by batteries, those lanterns are disappearing. This would be a good time to rehabilitate these lanterns as one of the traditional symbols of Macau, because while not being exclusive to Macau, it was in Macau that this type of lantern got refined and lasted until toaday. The design of the Macau Pavilion is inspired by the traditional Little Rabbit Lantern. It is a totally transparent case, without sharp corners and edges, with a smooth hair-spring ramp inside, embracing a passionate and vibrant heart (a simulator for 38 people) and dimmed partially on the top and by the sides by Solar Photovoltaic Louvers, finally topped by the moveable head and tail of the rabbit. All public spaces are totally free of architectural obstruction.

Located beside the Hong Kong and Taiwan Pavilions, the Macau Pavilion generously has one façade facing the main square, where various activities will take place, therefore the Macau Pavilion

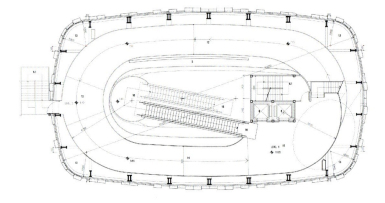

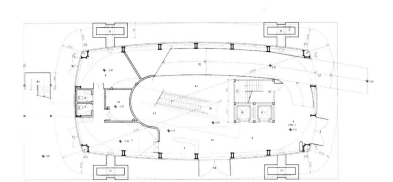

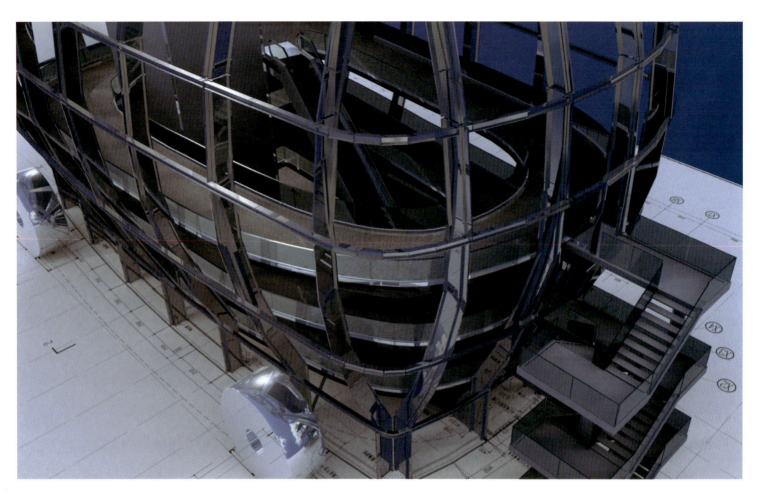

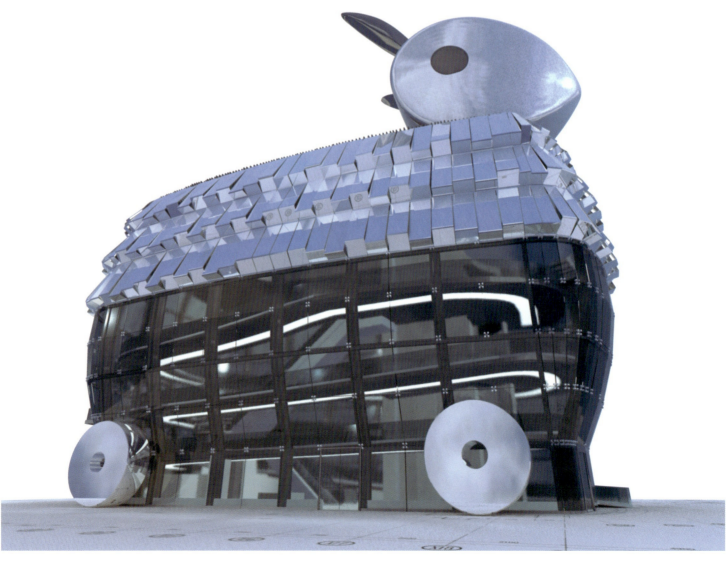

needs to be vibrant, dynamic, and maximising its front and above in order to be visible and attractive from short and long distances. Visitors are invited inside by welcome PR offering them colourful little rabbit lanterns. While moving up and down through the hair-spring exhibition ramps, visitors will create a global inter-activity with their lanterns and by touching on the multimedia surfaces. Advanced technologies for multimedia and interactive entertaining elements are projected on the outer surface of the simulator, partially on the floor of the ramps and on selected surfaces. This transforms the pavilion into a screen or gigantic hologram; in other words, it becomes a theatre in which visitors take the place of actors on the stage. The simulator is the central attraction and features one to three shows.

The Macau Pavilion is an environmentally friendly building because it uses clean energy building-integrated through Solar Photovoltaic Systems, without generator, reducing harmful gas emissions into the atmosphere; the complete super-structure is built in steel in order to save water, being the material totally dismountable and re-usable; the dirigible head and tail balloons will be manoeuvred by simple mechanisms. Last but not least, the Macau Pavilion does harmonise and echo the style of China National Pavilion because both are inspired by traditional elements and both are re-invented in a contemporary way.

The Macau Pavilion will arouse sympathy of audiences and the Little Rabbit Lantern will overrun all the corners of EXPO 2010 Shanghai.

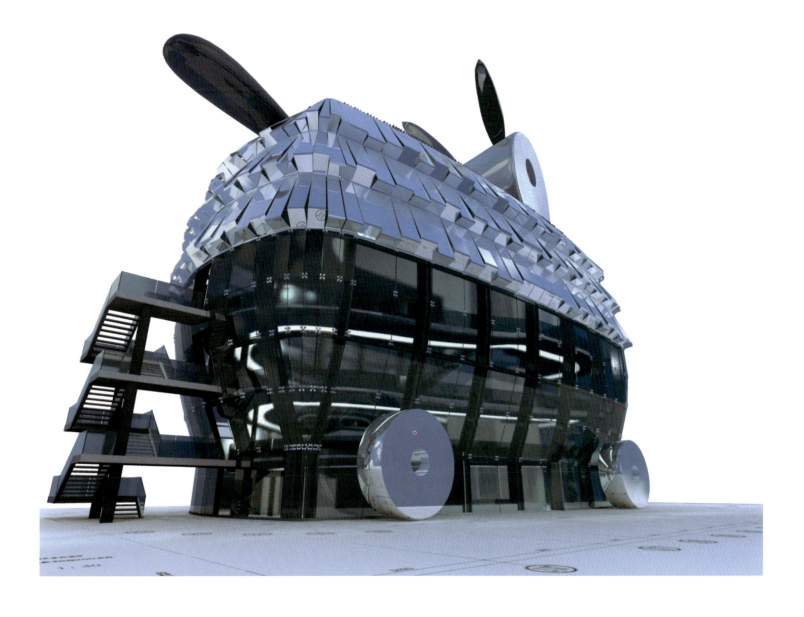

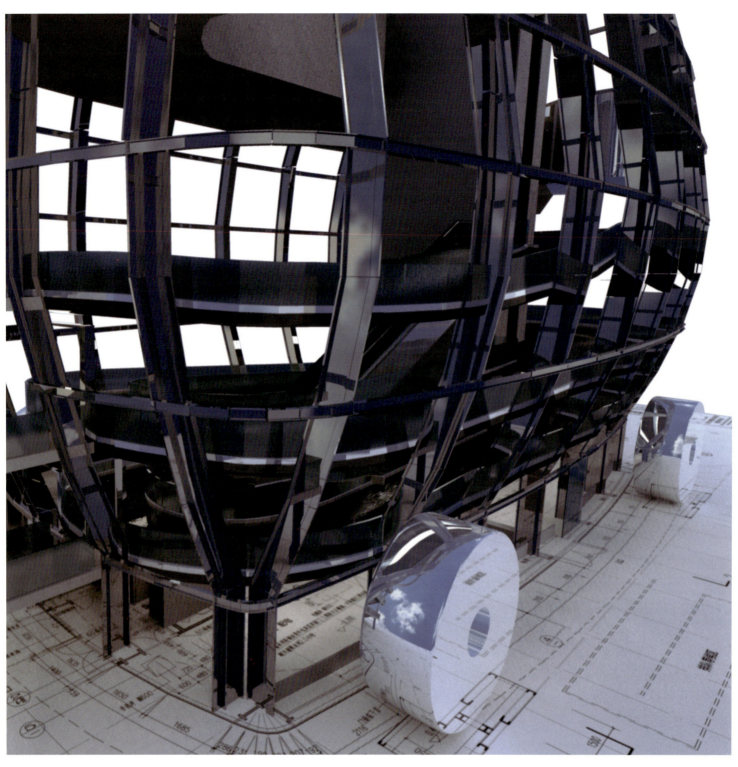

Shanghai EXPO 2010 Mexico Pavilion Competition

Project name: Mexico Pavilion Proposal **Designer:** AS Arquitectura **Place in the competition:** Entry to the final **Organiser:** Shanghai EXPO

Project Description:

The project's concept is strongly related to the Exposition's theme in which Mexico's urban history is presented as a positive design approach for the future cities of the world. This concept is expressed in the diagonal plaza, in which urban spaces of different Mexican eras are conceptualised as patios, designed in accordance to the time in history when these elements were used in Mexican cities. Aprehispanic promenade, a colonial plaza, the conformation of multiple cities of the 19th century and the global city of the 20th century area are all expressed in this part of the building. Inside these spaces, elements that reinterpret the urban and ecological values of these cities are shown as sculptural protagonists of the public space. Accordingly the Expositions related to the history are located around these spaces in the lower level.

The pavilion was conceived in a way that the construction materials can mostly be reutilised for other projects. The main structure is metallic, and the walls and ceilings are made from pre-cast concrete elements. All materials are integrated with their natural appearance. Structural and constructive honesty is the fundamental idea of the composition.

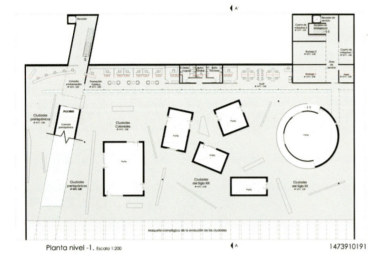

Planta nivel -1. Escala 1:200

1473910191

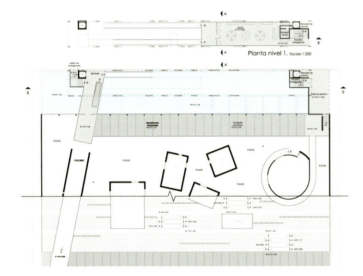

Planta nivel 1. Escala 1:200

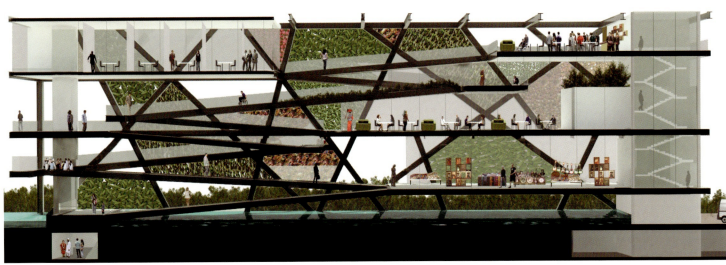

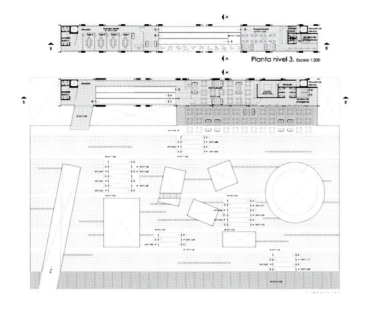

Planta nivel 3. Escala 1:200

Shanghai EXPO 2010 Mexico Pavilion Competition

Project name: Mexico Pavilion Proposal **Designer:** Serrano Monjaraz Arquitectos **Place in the competition:** Entry to the final

Project Description:

The building's concept was based on the selection of the main Mexican icon empathised in the facades in a contemporary way and combined with an important presence of natural elements. The interior design of the pavilion is based on the interior path that leads the visitor through all the areas. The entrance corridors are a series of ramps to make sure the access is comfortable for all visitors and to assure that the huge number of guests per day will not have long waiting lines under the sun or rain.

The journey starts from the access ramp where sounds, scents and perspective lead the way towards the main plaza on the second level. This outdoor area surprises visitors with the interaction of natural elements and representative volumes of Mexican architecture.

A descending ramp leads towards the permanent exhibit—a neutral space deluged with multimedia. Walking, standing, sitting or lying on the floor, the visitor may watch a multiple projection of a single video—with no start or end—presented in different sizes and positions throughout the area. A big bench, which symbolises the relation between the Chinese dragon and the Mexican serpent, is the marked spot where visitors can freely rest and leisure with the multimedia performance. The show presents the essence of Mexico in its main cities, their history, present and future.

Next the visitor enters the reference room with a series of interactive elements with relevant themes of Mexico, for those interested in an approach to the following subjects: geography, biodiversity, culture, tourism, etc. Following the temporal exhibits

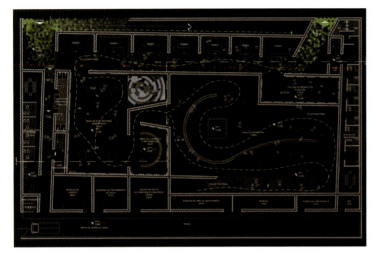

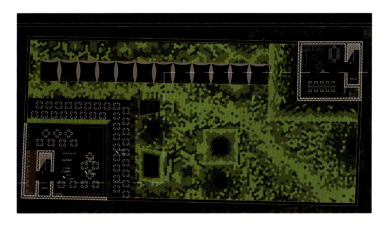

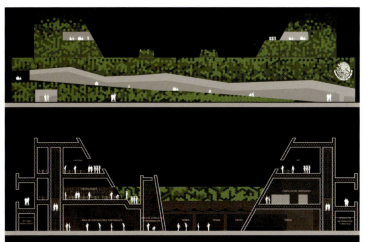

hall is found, a big patio with a water mirror fountain and the possibility of natural or artificial light, according to exhibit's needs. The final corridor leads to the exit through the store that recreates a "tianguis" a series of commercial spaces with typical Mexican arts and crafts. The business centre is linked to the west volume where the VIP lounge is located. It has magnificent views of the pavilion's interior plaza and panoramic views of the surrounding outdoors. The spaces are needed for the day to day operation where located the rest of the layout offices for the pavilion staff, access, service area, maintenance room, mechanical room and storage. In the interior of the east volume the restaurant was located, with the capacity for 21 tables in the 276 square metres interior and 34 tables in the 176 square metres terrace with views to the interior plaza of the pavilion. On the second level of the restaurant a Cantina (saloon) was located with an interior area and a terrace with fantastic views of the outdoors.

Shanghai EXPO 2010 Nepal Pavilion Competition

Project name: Nepal Pavilion–Nepal Araniko Centre **Designer:** Implementing Experts Group (IEG) of Kathmandu **Place in the competition:** Winner **Organiser:** The Government of Nepal **Theme:** Tales of Kathmandu City – Seeking the Soul of A City; Explorations and Speculations

Project Description:

At the 5.28 square kilometres EXPO site, the Nepal Pavilion will be built at a 3,600 square metres area which is located at the centre of the EXPO and in front of the Chinese National Pavilion. The Nepal Pavilion at the EXPO 2010 Shanghai will look like an ancient settlement that exists in and around Boudhnath Monastery in Kathmandu. In line with the theme of the EXPO 2010 – "Better City, Better Life", the Nepal Pavilion will focus on rapid urban development that is taking place in the ancient capital city of Kathmandu and the consequent impact on nature and environment. With the theme "Tales of Kathmandu City – seeking the soul of a city; explorations and speculations", the Nepal Pavilion will walk down the paths of history in search of the soul of the mystical city of Kathmandu and captures snapshots of magical moments of Kathmandu as a centre of art, architecture and cultural excellences. The pavilion presents urban development and translates into an architectural form to express understanding of the city as it was at the time of Araniko, the famous Nepalese architect and as it is now. Vibrant urban spaces of Kathmandu will be created by the very nature of its "architectural style and space concepts" that have developed in Nepal for more than 2,000 years.

Following the main theme of the EXPO 2010, a vision for the future will be explored through the critical overview of the past and the integration and developmental aspects of urbanism. Likewise, Nepalese presentation at the EXPO 2010 will highlight efforts to protect environment and renewal energy and also present green architecture as the future architectural direction.

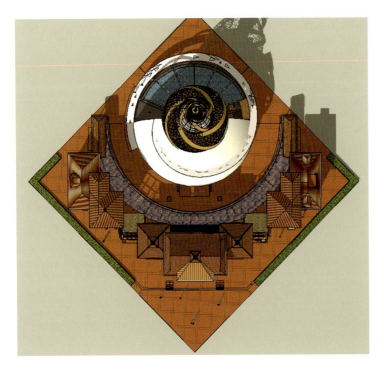

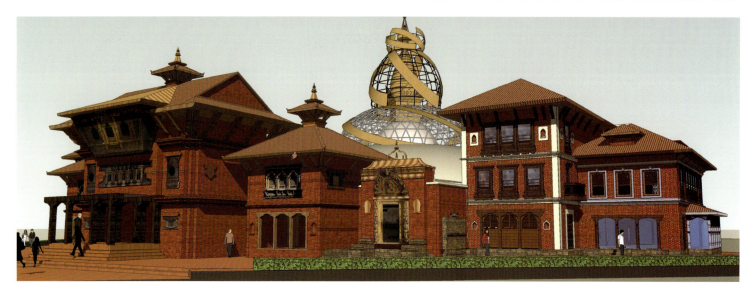

Age old hierarchical harmony between two major world philosophies – Buddhism and Hinduism, which flourish hand in hand in Nepal, will also be reflected in the architectural grandeur of the Nepal Pavilion. The pavilion landscape and garden will resemble the essence and contents of picturesque natural settings dotted with the highest peak on earth – the Mt. Everest, Lumbini, which is the birthplace of Buddha, spiral of green mountains and valleys and tranquil peaceful glacier lakes and rivers. Numerous Nepalese indigenous flowers will blossom at the Peace Gardens of Nepal Pavilion. To present ambience and atmosphere of Nepal at the EXPO 2010, several important Nepalese festivals and fairs will also be organised with the participation of native artists, musicians and dancers from Nepal.

The entire carving works in wood, metal and stone are produced in Kathmandu by local skilled carvers and will be transported to Shanghai for the construction of the Nepal Pavilion. Expert Nepalese craftsmen and carpenters will travel to Shanghai EXPO site to erect the majestic national Pavilion of Nepal.

Shanghai EXPO 2010
The Netherlands Pavilion
Competition

Project name: The Netherlands Pavilion — Happy Street **Designer:** John Kormeling **Place in the competition**: Winner **Organiser**: Ministry for Economic Affairs/ i.o. EVD **Theme:** Happy Street

Project Description:

"Better City, Better Life", the theme of the EXPO 2010, is originated from a good street. The name of the Dutch Pavilion is Happy Street.A street with different types of buildings such as houses, shops, factories, offices, city-farms, petrol stations, and sport fields, forms the condition for a social life.

The pavilion is a street of 450-metre long, of a wonderful steel construction poetry for the mind. The space is in the shape of "8". The colour of the street is red, while the beautiful Dutch architecture is white,except one building—three years ago at the former EXPO site, John Kormeling saw a nice Chinese house, and it will be built again at the Happy Street. The VIP room is a big yellow THANK YOU Shanghai crown building. This will be a funny Dutch pavilion made in China. Covered with sparkling LED's, the pavilion is a fake, but the real stuff will be exhibited inside.

There is an imitation polder with sheep, a soft-sitting-landscape. The restaurant is composed of a cutterhead of a dredger. On its roof, light-words say cloud, sand, sun...You can pull a meatball out of the wall. There will be a billboard house and a souvenir shop.

The world EXPO is a centre for pleasure, amusement, and education. So the Dutch Pavilion is like a walkable rollercoaster with buildings hanging on it like apples on a tree.

In each building along the road, there is something to see, an invention, a product, a sculpture or a secret which makes life more

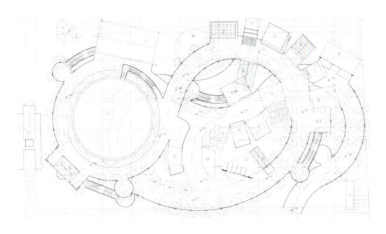

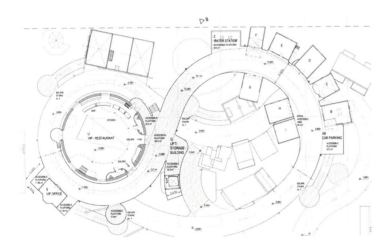

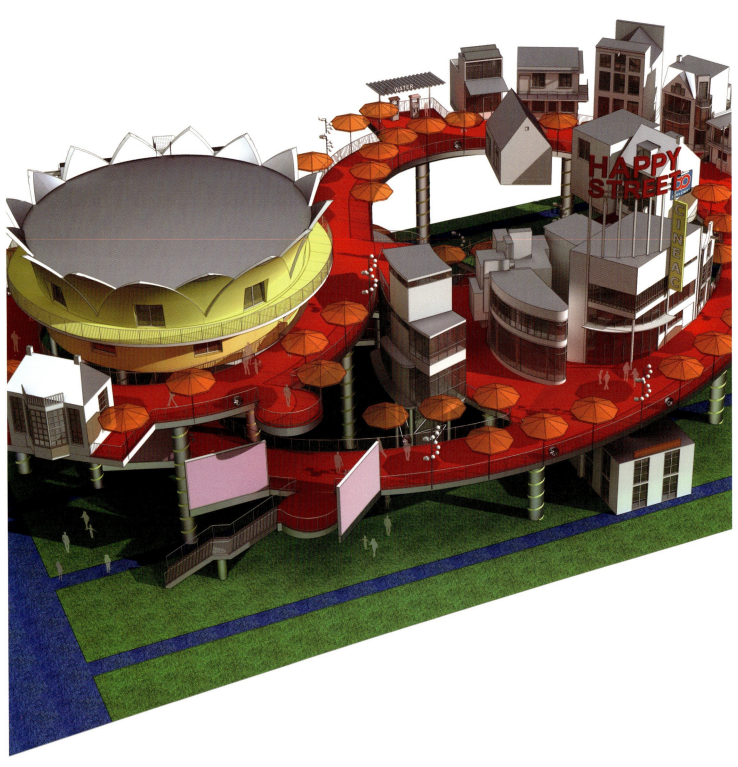

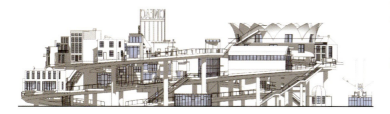

joyful, with new ways of energy, growing food and purification of water. The architect wants to make an open pavilion with no door where the interior is outside.

The concept is regarded as innovative and controversial, because it is not a pavilion but a spatial public area proposed. Most importantly, China understood this layered street.

Shanghai EXPO 2010 Norway Pavilion Competition

Project name: Norway Pavilion **Designer:** Helen & Hard **Place in the competition:** Winner **Organiser:** Norway Government **Theme:** Norway Powered by Nature

Project Description:

EXPO 2010 Shanghai is the first World Fair to adopt sustainable urban development as its theme. This sort of ambition must promote concepts which restrict the extensive resource use and big investments which a World Fair involves. The basic concept of "Norway powered by Nature" lies in precisely this challenge, placing emphasis on the awareness of several aspects of sustainability. The explosive urbanisation which China is experiencing calls for increased sensibility and consideration for human and natural resources. "Norway powered by Nature" contributes to this issues with investigations in sustainable infrastructure, healthy public recreational areas and environmentally friendly urban structures. Sustainable future use is not just about re-using materials but about an understanding of long-term cycles. That is why the pavilion is a prefabricated building kit consisting of 15 "trees" constructed in timber. Each of the trees, as well as the exhibition, can be easily dismantled and erected after EXPO at other locations, for example, a shaded park, a playground and a social meeting place. Awareness of sustainability implies synergetic linking of different disciplines, cultures and development processes to create a new whole. This new whole is expressed as an evocative and heterogeneous landscape, which combines Norwegian and Chinese culture, commerce, technology and art, various forms of interaction and experiences, as well as interpretations of Norwegian nature in relation to city development. Each tree functions at the same time as construction, infrastructure (air-condition, water-purification, energy supply, lighting, etc.), furniture, exhibition,

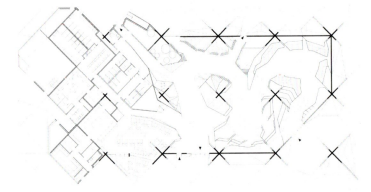

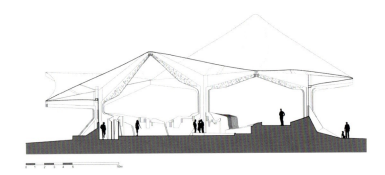

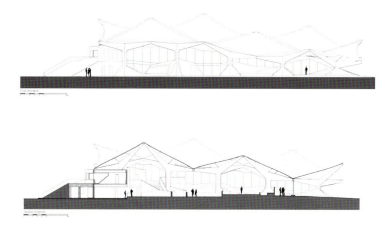

playground and information-display. All these requirements are intertwined in a multifunctional structure.

The choice of laminated timber for the main construction has been made with an eye to little impact on the environment. Each "tree" consists of a fabric roof, four "branches", a "trunk" and "roots". The components of the 15 "trees" can be packed flat to make optimal use of space and transportation. A recently-developed timber-product in China, GluBam—Glue-laminated Bamboo—will be used for secondary supporting structures, the exhibition and most of the surfaces in the pavilion. The roof of the pavilion is a four point sail-membrane construction. The fabric provides shade against direct sunlight while letting light in and thereby saving energy for interior lighting. The fabric reduces structural bulk, and is easy to transport and re-use.

The pavilion has a low-energy concept with systems such as solar panels, water collection and adjustable air vents, integrated into the architecture and part of the exhibition. Norway is in the forefront of water purification technology and these systems can be used to purify rainwater. The purification process of rainwater which is collected on the roof is made visible and understandable to the public, who can drink cooled, clean water from open taps. The ventilation system uses natural motive power (chimney effect plus wind).

Shanghai EXPO 2010 Poland Pavilion Competition

Project name: Poland Pavilion **Designer:** WWA Architects **Place in the competition:** Winner **Organiser:** Polish Information and Foreign Investment Agency **Theme:** Human Creates City

Project Description:

Project Concept

In the contemporary world with its abundance of visual experience, with the pictorial language of communication reigning supreme, with the almost unconstrained and instant accessibility of iconographic material, an Exposition piece of architecture will only be attractive insofar as it can offer perceptual sensations attainable only through direct, unmediated exposure to out-of-the-ordinary, singular stimuli, insofar as it can provide a quality of experience born out of the chemistry of inter-sensory stimulation. Given the nature of the Exposition, the exhibition facility has to denote, by its aesthetic distinctiveness, the country of origin, has to constitute, by the strength of its stylistic connotations, an evocative, recognisable and memorable cultural ideogram. In the design, the cultural idiom is primarily conveyed through the theme, the motif of folk-art paper cut-out, or, more precisely, through a rendering of the motif, a transcription of an elementary aesthetic code into the contemporary language of architectural décor. The transcription rationale was twofold. First of all, the architects did not wish the design to be a literal folklore, a mechanical multiplication of convention-approved set patterns. The intention was for the structure décor to draw on and make reference to tradition, but ultimately to be that tradition's contemporary reinterpretation, a creative extension into the present day by way of inspiration rather than replication. Secondly, the designers aspired to make the structure in its own right, in a purely architectural dimension, a significant landmark, a showcase of Polish design achievements. It should be an attractive, eye-

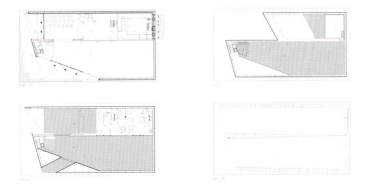

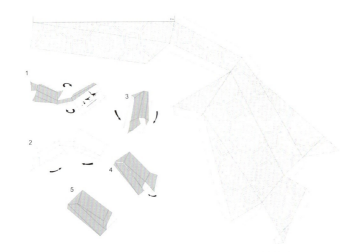

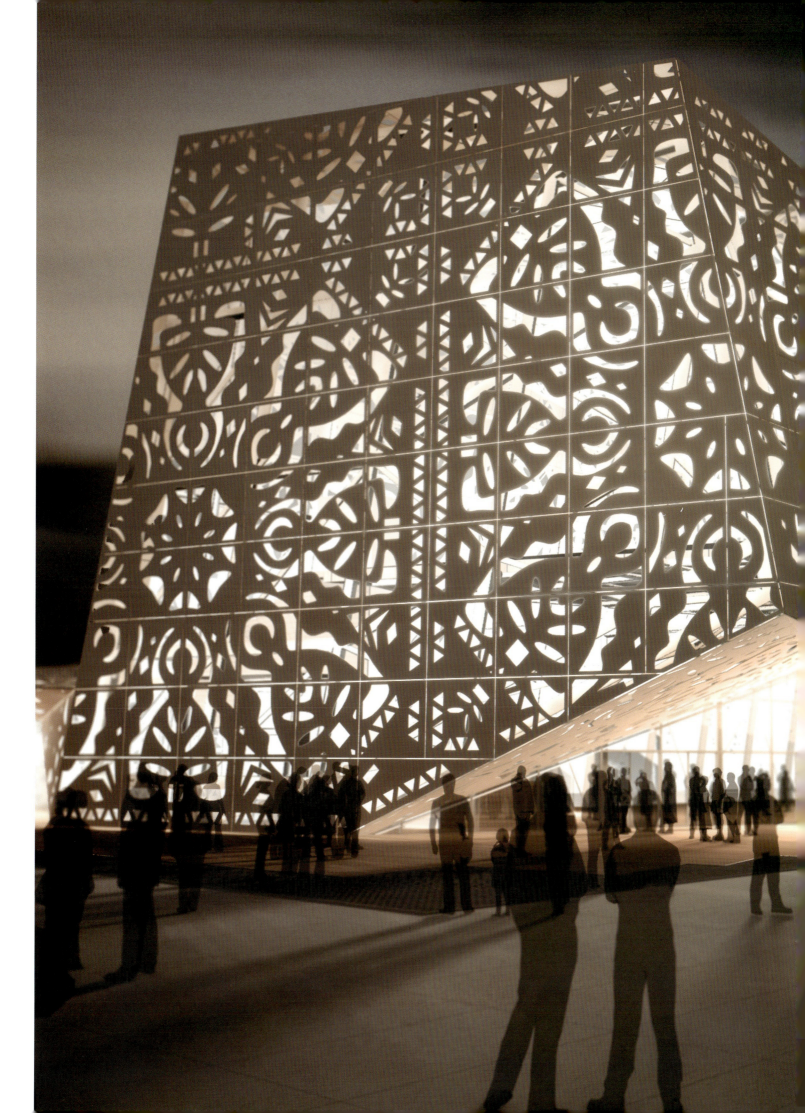

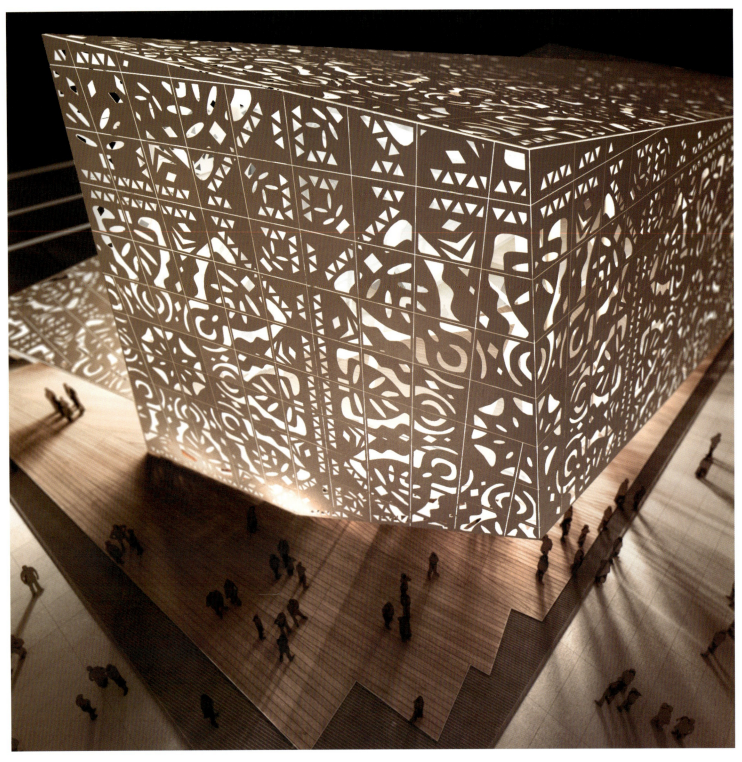

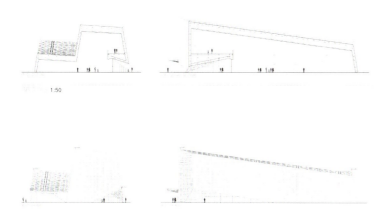

1:50

catching exterior both in daylight, against the panorama of other EXPO facilities, as well as a mesmerizing experience at night with the edifice drawn by the multicoloured light seeping through the cut-out patterns. Reversely, it should provide inside visitors with comparable experience by shaping the outer skin patterning in such a way that the sun rays shining through would chisel, by light and shade, the space under the vault. The structure's overall shape, with many slanting planes, on the one hand complements and rounds out, by the suggestion of a folded sheet of paper-the "cut-out" narrative; on the other hand, it creates inside a geometrically intriguing and flexible space that can be creatively apportioned, by inner divisions, to different exhibitions, performances and utility functions and uses.

Functional Arrangements

The outside structure of the pavilion and its reflection in the proposed arrangement of its inside functions impose on the visitors taking and following a route which is consistent with the logic of the building. The entranceway—an interlude between an inside and outside body of the construction—is accessible from the square marked out between the pavilions. The partial roof created by the

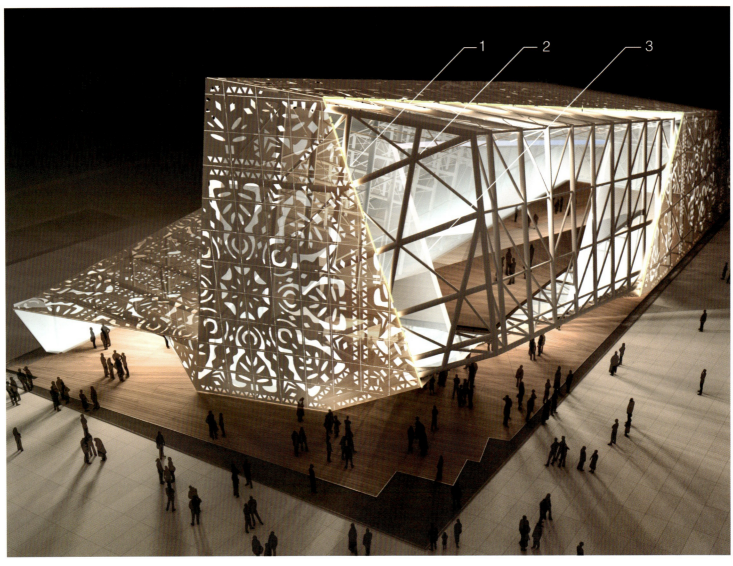

fold in the building allows for arranging an open-air restaurant as well as for providing the queues of visitors with a shelter from an elements. The entrance opens onto the hall containing the information centre, a restaurant and a shop. Next visitors proceed to the main, full-height exhibition area of the pavilion. It is the space painted with the light filtering through the cut-out patterns of the elevation, creating a "chiaroscuro" effect. Consequently, the interior of the building will create a background for scheduled performances and presentations, e.g. directly connected with depicting the life of a typical Polish city. Auxiliary functions have been designed in the lowest part of the building, under the ramp leading onto the rooftop. Continuing the route, visitors enter the area of the exhibition, devoted to the future of the cities. The wooden, ground-level floor is gradually rising, acquiring the form of terraced stairs and becoming an auditorium for performances taking place below. The stairs take visitors onto the mezzanine, where exhibitions of Polish regions are to be located. Visitors on their way to the exit would pass by a restaurant and a shop.

Material Solutions

The outer layer of the elevation, with its characteristic design inspired by a traditional folk-art paper cut-out, is made of impregnated CNC plotter-cut plywood mounted on steel construction modules with steel substructure. Panel wall elements PC are mounted on the outer side of the modules. The exterior, entranceway surface and the interior of the pavilion will all be covered with impregnated wooden flooring. The choice of materials and the character of construction were to a large extent dictated by the idea of possible future reclaiming and recycling of the pavilion structure or its parts, e.g. by reconstructing it in one of the Polish cities after the closing of EXPO. The colouristic effects were determined by the choice of plywood panels in natural wood colour.

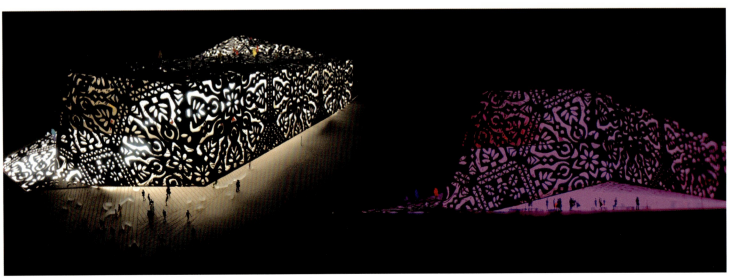

As dusk falls, the elevation will acquire different colours according to the changes of light penetrating the cut-out patterns.

Shanghai EXPO 2010 Poland
Pavilion Competition

Project name: Poland Pavilion Proposal **Designer:** Ingarden & Ewy Architects **Place in the competition:** Entry to the final

Project Description:

The main idea underlying the design is to create a unique and unconventional dictionary of architecture, which will allow references to the "Better City, Better Life" main theme of EXPO 2010 and at the same time will create an image of modern Poland understandable to the Chinese and international community. This will be achieved through:

The Town—the Poland Pavilion is a reflection of the spatial code of the Polish town

The design of the Poland Pavilion proposes a synthetic presentation of spaces typical of the major Polish cities with medieval origins—i.e. having a main market square. The zone is to create, similarly to existing layouts of Polish cities, a main public area deciding the character of the place, and in the case of the pavilion, introducing the visitor to the exhibition space.

Frédéric Chopin and Folk Music Inspirations

Cut-out, a folk art motif—original element unspotted in this form outside of Poland, is an element which, when adapted in architecture, is to create a new quality—as in Chopin's music, combining folk traditions with modernity. The use of the form of a cut-out, its open-work patterns and bends of the plain, to create a clear landmark and structure of the building works well for the design in a surprisingly natural manner.

Signs in the City—Multimedia Projections

The expression of the "city space" of the pavilion is strengthened by multimedia projections, which are accompanied by zonal sound effects. There will be digitally processed projections on the walls of

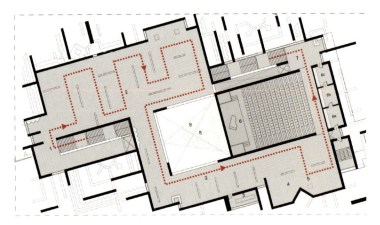

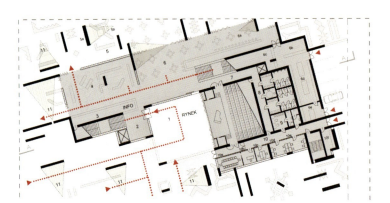

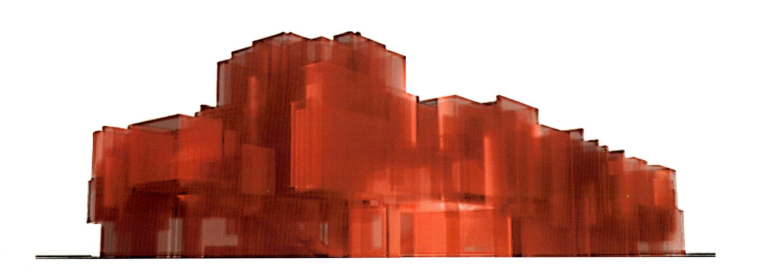

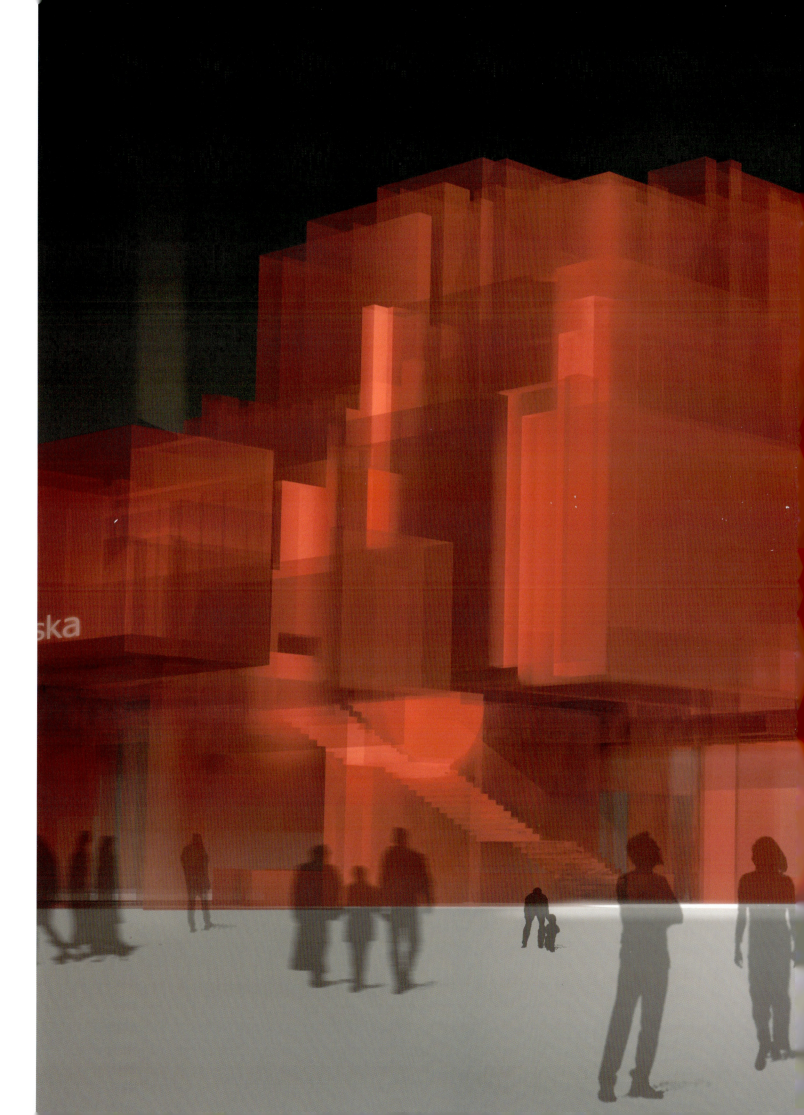

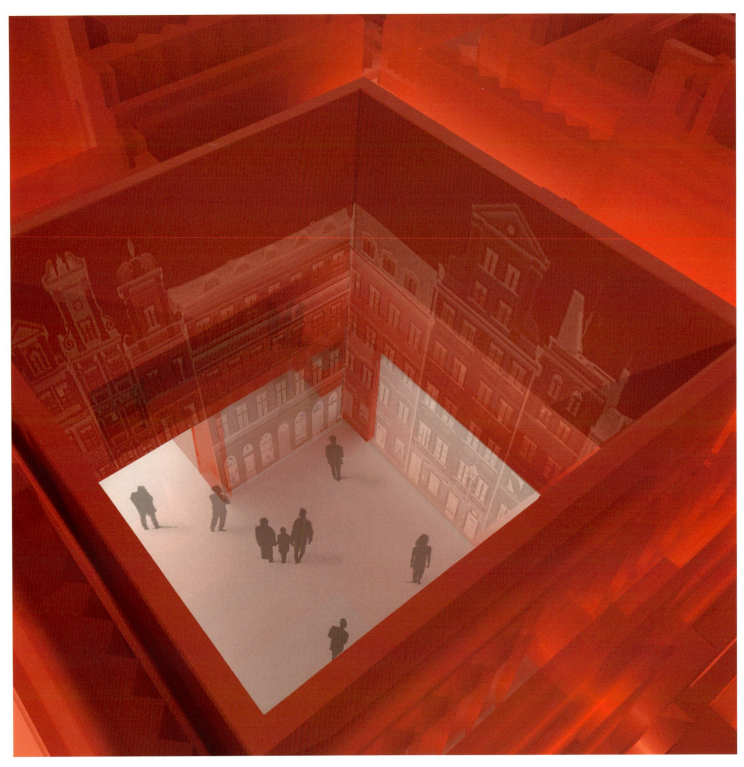

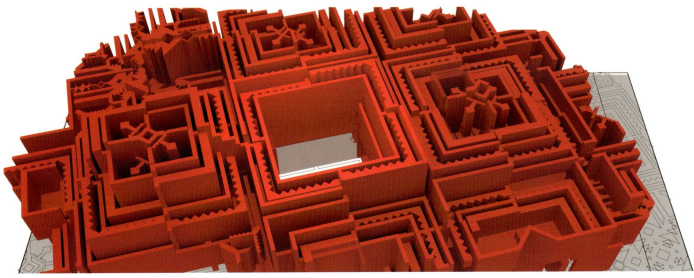

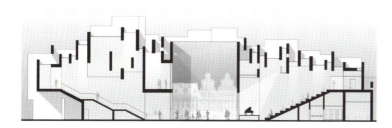

the building—images of life in Polish cities. Virtual people walking against the background of old city houses of Gdańsk, Poznań and Kraków will merge with real visitors. The presentation of famous, historic figures and of modern communities is in response to the "People make the city" theme.

The proposed colours of the pavilion are shades of red. The colour of the image projection areas will change (reduction of the LED lighting to produce matte white as a kind of screens for the projections). The rhythm of the unique architectural screens in precisely defined places is to indicate the course to be followed when visiting the exhibition.

Modern Art Deco

The selected design also makes a reference to the achievements of the Polish architecture and the tradition of world exhibitions. Mention must be made here of the Poland Pavilion in Paris erected in 1925 (architectural design by J. Czajkowski, interior paintings inter alia by Zofia Stryjeńska) in the Polish Art Deco style.

Recycling – The Main Theme

Skeletal steel structure covered with panels was made of modern recycled plastics (e.g. PANELITE). The synthetic materials used in the design were selected on the basis of their transparency grading. They range from fully transparent components, with sources of light in-between, used in the public spaces, to fully opaque components combined with sound-proof materials in spaces requiring proofing, such as the concert hall and some of the exhibitions. The floors will be made of non-abrasive epoxy resin.

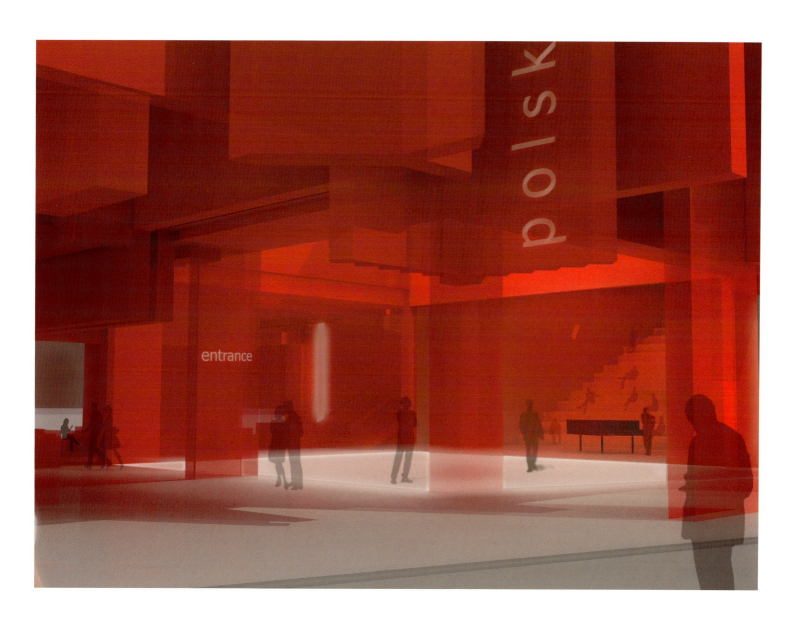

Shanghai EXPO 2010 Russia Pavilion Competition

Project name: Russia Pavilion **Designer:** "P. A. P. E. R. architectural Team"
Place in the competition: Winner **Organiser:** Stock company All-Russia Exhibition Centre (AREC) **Theme:** New Russia: City and People

Project Description:
The building comprises a multitude of interconnected objects. Every single object conveys its distinctive ideological message and is, at the same time, integrated into the literary tissue of the building.

The design of the pavilion is akin to ancient Slavic prototypes and structures such as Stonehenge. Its shape symbolises the flower of life, the sun, and the roots of the "World Tree" (a colossal oak-tree in the Slavic mythology) supporting Heaven on its branches.

The lower platform of the pavilion symbolises the basis of life, cultural and historical roots, memory of people and their connection with the previous generations and with nature. The whole of the lower part of the platform is covered with a species of shingle that Russian craftsmen have used since time immemorial.

The white and gold of the towers is an allusion to the historical images of Russian architecture, and the red background serves to enliven the perforation of the tower's upper parts. The perforation patterns are based on ethnic motifs and symbols of Russia's different peoples. RED has always been associated with the idea of beauty, while GOLD is a symbol of prosperity and WHITE, a symbol of purity and spirituality.

The lower part of the pavilion with a spectators' amphitheatre is an image of a city square where horizontal parts of L-shaped towers are gathered towards the centre and where a panorama of the installation "City of Flowers" opens to the eye.

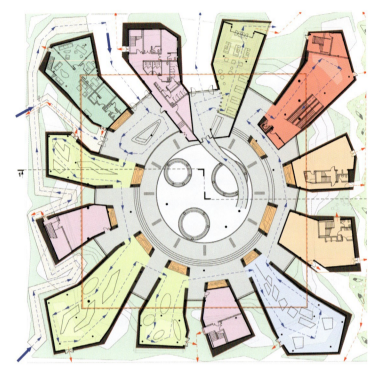

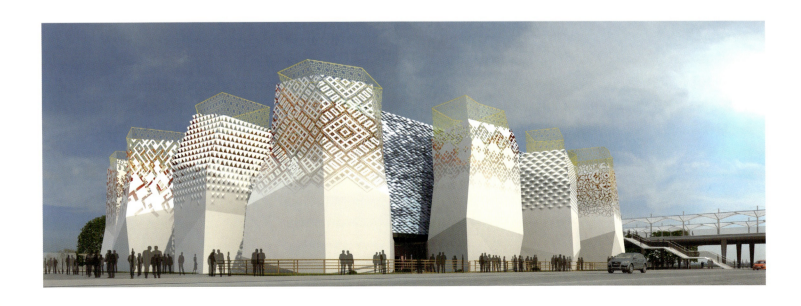

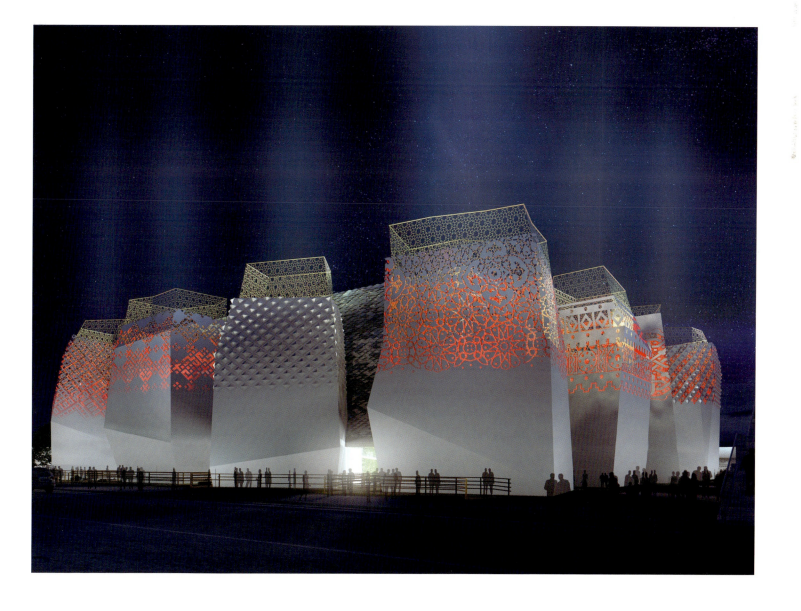

Shanghai EXPO 2010 Serbia Pavilion Competition

Project name: Serbia Pavilion **Designer:** Ana Kovencz - Vujić, Ksenija Bulatović, Andreja Mitrović, Miloš Živković, Daniela Perović **Place in the competition:** Winner **Organiser:** SIEPA (Serbia Investment and EXPOrt Promotion Agency) **Theme:** Belgrade, the City of Rivers, Leisure and Parks

Project Description:

The Serbian thread is the main theme of this year's EXPO, which represents a symbolic symbiosis, a harmonious fusion of the new and old, and of the deeply rooted and newly planted. It uses this symbol as a metaphor for the concept of sustainable development, cohabitation, and the creativity of citizens of Serbian cities and their aspiration to continuously improve both themselves and the cities they live in.

A longer façade will exhibit subtly the national identity of the pavilion and the most significant brand of Serbia: achievements of Nikola Tesla. The fasade faces the road, with a digital screen displaying four fields: sports, culture, history and economy. The fasade about the entrance is designed with grey inscription on white glass of the names of celebrities written in grey colour. Automatic catapulting of a continuously moving fluorescent ball symbolises a tennis ball on an artificially verdant roof, bouncing from one side to the other, visible from afar, which will certainly draw attention to the facility itself.

Across a water channel, symbolising the Danube and connection with the world, the visitor enters the pavilion. The main theme appears already in the waiting hall at the entrance to the pavilion: new better Serbia, better new Belgrade. The message is Belgrade, the city of rivers, leisure and parks.

On the west wall is a big orthophoto footage of Belgrade, emphasising water and green areas and New Belgrade, which will celebrate its 62nd birthday during the EXPO. On the north wall are some displays of old Belgrade, animation of the Belgrade fortress

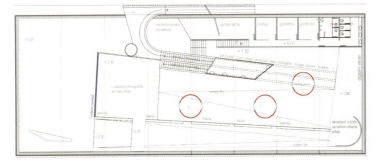

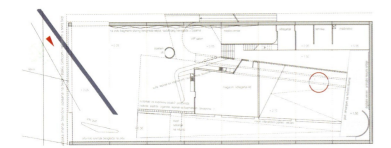

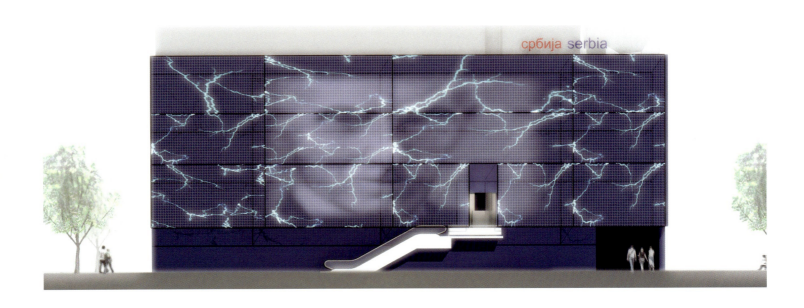

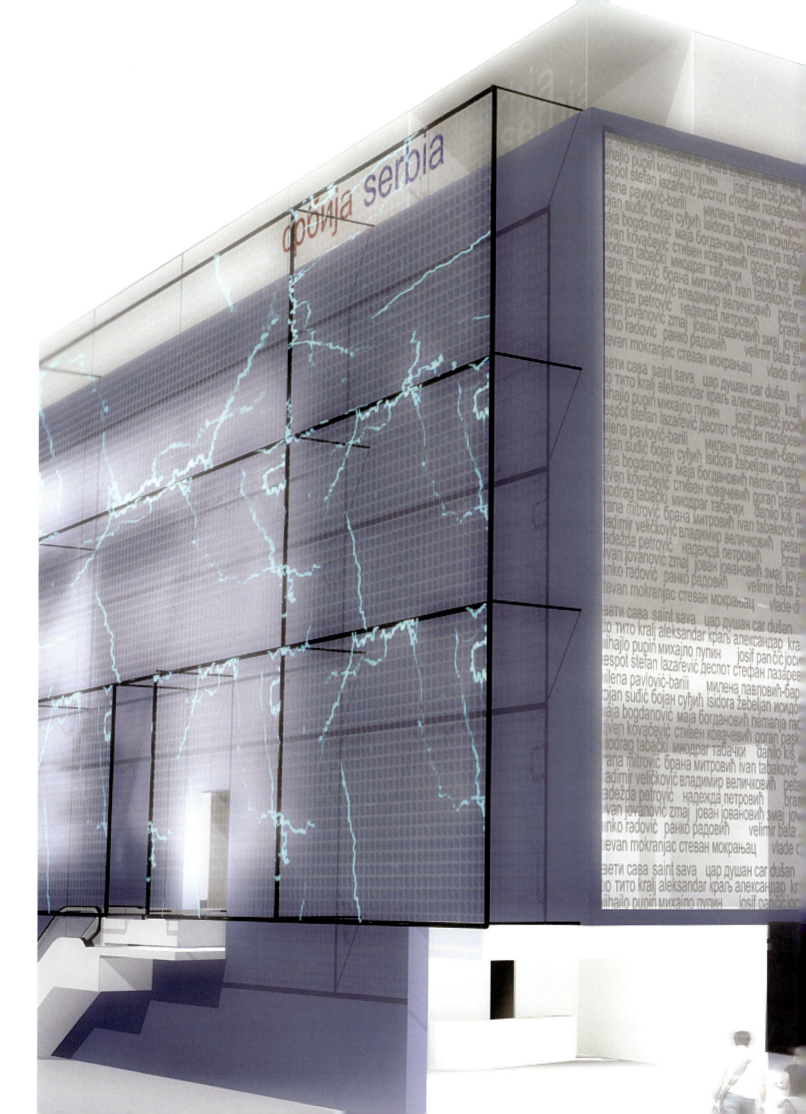

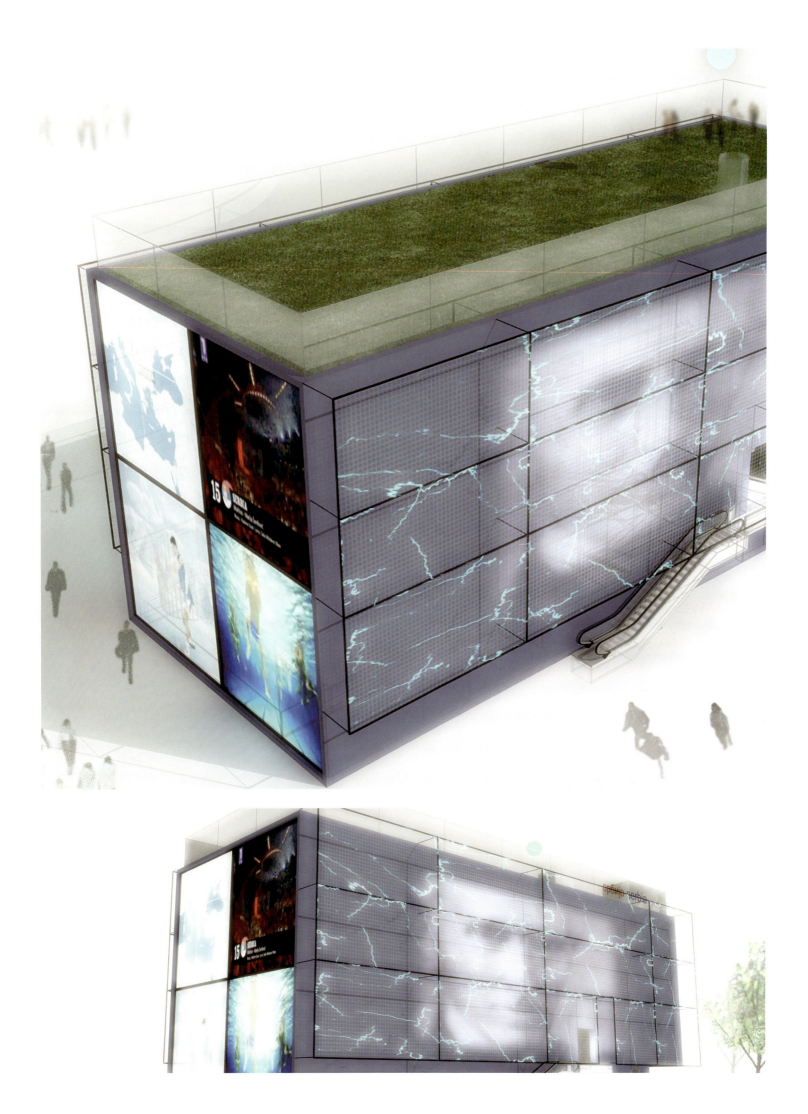

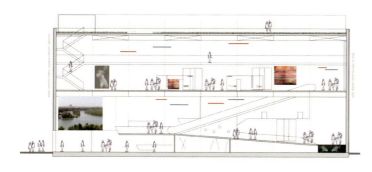

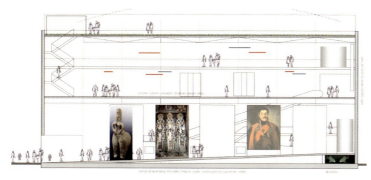

in alteration dynamic displaying of parks, the Great War Island, Belgrade life pulsating, souvenirs with the theme of Serbia, etc. The design elements for displaying Serbian identity interactively mean the involvement of all senses including sight, hearing, smell, taste, and touch. Firstly, the architects clearly define the flow of numerous visitors between static pictures, photographs on one side and dynamic, digital and interactive displays on the other side of the envisaged trajectory for visitors, involving visitors by action and interactive screens and games. Secondly, individual, few, but carefully selected objects are on display, for instance, paintings, sculptures, national costumes, endemic species of flora and fauna in visitors' direct field of vision. Thirdly, the theme nuclei is in form of a 3-metre diameter roll, 3.5-metre high, with two narrow passages, serving visitors who want to get completely immersed in some typical themes and atmosphere... Fourthly, big digital and static screens on the walls display important elements, people, appearances at the choice of editor and author. Fifthly, music, light installations, water sounds act as animation. And finally, activities for visitors' involvement are provided.

Shanghai EXPO 2010 Serbia Pavilion Competition

Project name: Serbia Pavilion Proposal **Designer:** Nikola Arsenic, Ueslei Bonin, Henrique Gonçalves **Place in the competition:** Entry to the final

Project Description:

The Pavilion of the Republic of Serbia has been planned to be an open, interactive space of the exhibiting character and with free access. With its specific form treatment and materialisation, with its relation between the transparent base and the massive block above, it creates tension which provokes curiosity and interest in revealing its contents and getting to know them. The dark monolithic block with its irregular rims panelled with "granite" plaques suggests the steadiness and solidity of the genuine forms of the basic material, older than any of today's political concepts or of those in the past, not ever losing its essence.

"Floating" above the basic level on which people move it gives access from all sides and for all. It is erected above the transparent staircases with glass stairs which symbolically and instinctively suggest an invitation to go upstairs to the "upper" interactive level of the exhibiting character. There, when the visitor starts walking, the electronic signal activates video information which is instantly projected from the plaques in the central, internal part of the monolith as of the most intimate part, the heart of the "Balkan rock". While walking the visitor chooses unmarked areas and intuitively gets acquainted with the natural and cultural wealth, the technical potentials, the history and outstanding individuals of Serbia…
as well as hopes and expectations, modern views and the future people long for. All this is basically linked with cities and countries which represent the scenes of the contemporary life.

The successive change of pictures, which is a powerful and universal form of communication, makes visitors wish to stay longer

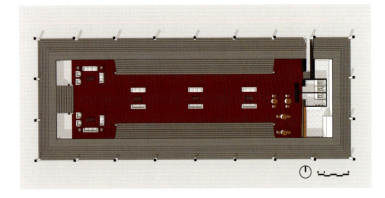

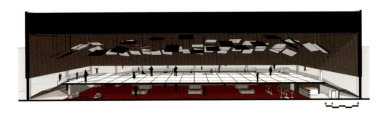

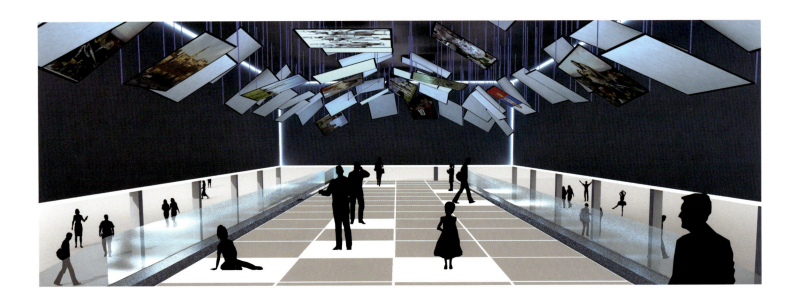

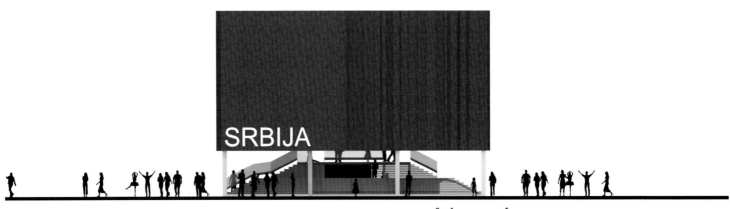

SRBIJA

0 1 5

in that central, lifted part of the pavilion, thus promoting it into a modern agora.

The level of the ground floor can be seen from far away but the access to it is suggested only when the use of the stairs going up is initiated. In one part there are a kitchen, sanitary facilities and management premises and VIP parlours for visitors with specific interests in business and other forms of cooperation. In the central part of the ground floor there are also places to degust the national dishes and beverages. On both levels there is a special access for the handicapped either through a directly cut-in entrance into the ground floor level or by a platform lift to the interactive exhibit space.

There are two marks of national identity. The first is the word "Srbija" in Serbian, in the low left hand corner of the front façade, "carved into the monolith" and lit by white, interior, indirect light. The second is the "Serbian three-colour flag" with a metallic wavy roof in colour for easier orientation, identification and marketing of the pavilion by means of digital browser and programmes such as Google Earth.

The designers would very much like to present one possible scenario for the message they want to send to the world: To create a better life in better cities, it is imperative to have a democratic space orientated towards connecting ideas, making new friends and strengthening associations. Serbia wants to be that space. The unison of these entireties of a polyvalent character in this unique space project contributes to the easier understanding of its democratic significance as a universal language of people, cities and nations.

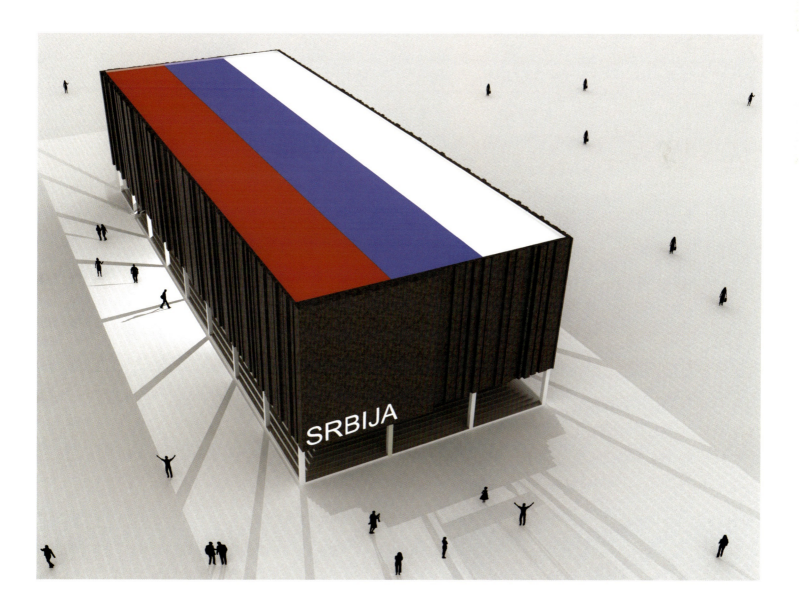

Shanghai EXPO 2010 Singapore Pavilion Competition

Project name: Singapore Pavilion **Designer:** Kay Ngee Tan Architects
Place in the competition: Winner **Organiser:** Singapore Tourism Board
Theme: Urban Symphony

Project Description:
The Singapore Pavilion at the Shanghai World EXPO in 2010 is to be called Urban Symphony, a tribute to Singapore where a delicate harmony of cultures exists in a city-state. The theme is best expressed in the architecture of the pavilion that resembles a musical box. It is an orchestra of elements – from the water fountain movements on the plaza, to the rhythm of fenestrations on the façade, to the interplay of sounds and visuals on the different levels, to the mélange of flora on the roof garden.

Water and Garden, the two elements of the design concept, not only form the softscape of the pavilion, they are two environmental issues Singapore has successfully tackled in its development, delicately balancing progress with sustainability.

The four columns supporting the entire structural system and the floors of the pavilion are different in shapes and sizes. They symbolise the four main races of the country living, working and playing happily on the same ground.

The visitor's experience will be a symphony to the senses. The ground floor is relatively open. Visitors and passersby can see directly into the heart of the ground floor from afar. Projected images and the live theatre will be located here, as well as up in mid air, making the high volume space even more dramatic.

The breathtaking structure has the upper floors that are cantilevered off the four columns.

Ramps and stairs leading to these upper floors are also suspended off trusses, to achieve a structural balance that has been intelligently achieved by Arup Engineers.

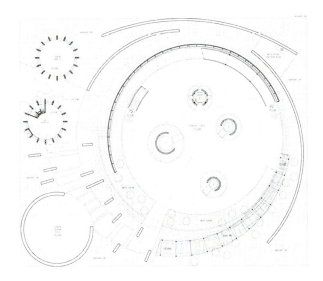

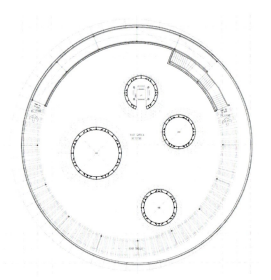

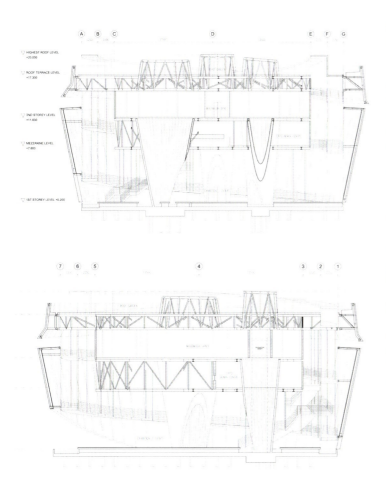

Most of the building materials, such as steel for the structural framework and aluminium panels for the façade, can be recycled after the EXPO. The foundation is designed with spun piles, other than columns, thus on the ground floor there will be no reinforced concrete.

Visitors stroll their way up the ramp, as in Guggenheim Museum in New York City. Exhibits and pictures on Singapore will be on display. Visitors can also enjoy the atrium space and activities in the main hall below before moving on to the second floor.

The second floor of about 600 square metres is column-free. In this ambient open space, there are three amphitheatres of different sizes, where visitors can gather to watch video performances of Singaporean pop artistes. This special feature highlights a creative subculture of Singapore rarely seen outside the country.

The pavilion shares a public square with countries from Oceania and can be viewed from various directions—from the 10 metre pedestrian walkway and the awesome Lu Po Grand Bridge which links the newly developed Pu-Dong to the ancient Pu-Xi .

The architecture has fully exploited these vantage points and resulted in a design that is like a sculpture in a landscaped square. The foreground of the square will give visitors the first taste of the Garden City. It is full of plants, and when activated, musical fountains will cool down the hot summer afternoons of Shanghai. Singapore's much-admired garden city also takes shape on the roof.

Shanghai EXPO 2010 Spain Pavilion Competition

Project name: Spain Pavilion **Designer:** Benedetta Tagliabue **Place in the competition:** Winner **Organiser:** SEEI (State Society for International Exhibitions) **Theme:** City for Generations

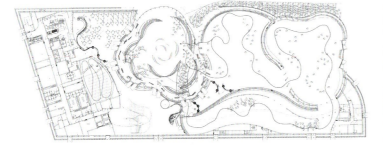

Project Description:

The project proposed by EMBT consists of developing the handicraft technique of the wicker into the practice of construction. With this goal in mind, the universal language of material works to build a bridge between East and West, and between Spain and China. With the volumetric, material, and structural inspirations of a wicker basket array, the void of the stands will mould a pavilion in which tubular metallic supports will sustain a wicker grid to filter the light and function as a climatic membrane that wraps the pavilion. "An EXPO is about national identity and about knowing and mixing", says Tagliabue. "So we would like some of the pavilion made in Spain and some in China or Asia. Wicker technology is the same across the world".

Essentially the plan is for panels of woven pillow stems which will be hung as a skin from the bones of steel supports. The pavilion is conceived as a series of baskets, some open at the top and some enclosed, creating a dappled light in courtyards, circulation and multipurpose spaces.

The colours of the wicker—from red brown to white—will be achieved by the treatments it would naturally go though: stripping, maintaining the skin, and treating to make it more durable.

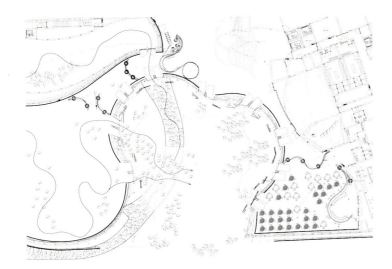

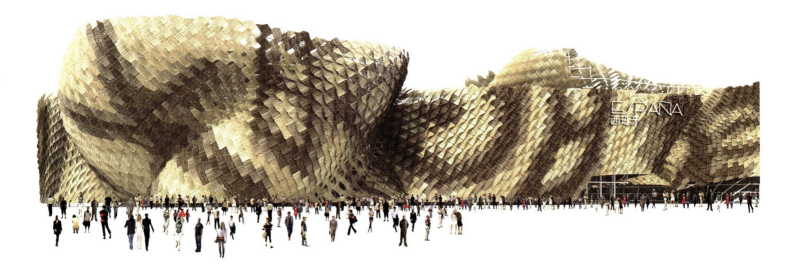

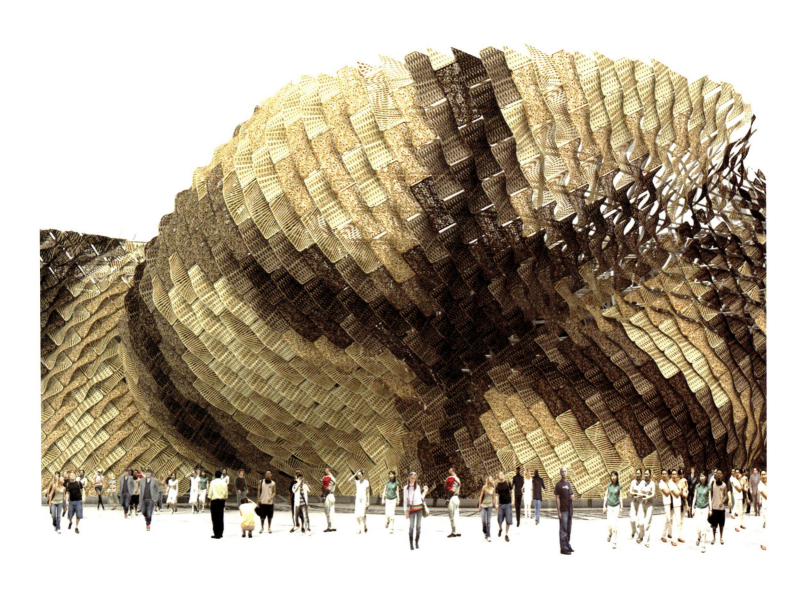

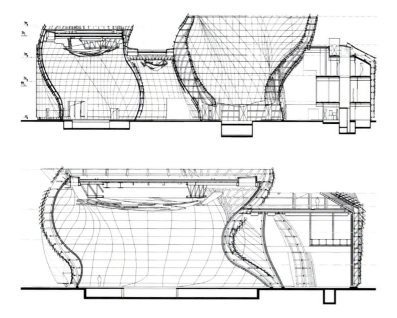

Shanghai EXPO 2010 Spain Pavilion Competition

Project name: Spain Pavilion Proposal **Designer:** [ecosistema urbano] architects ltd. **Place in the competition:** Entry to the final

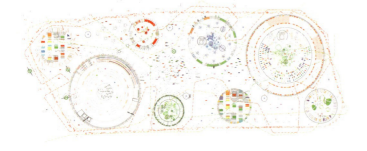

Project Description:

Spain Open City

The city is an ecosystem formed by the contact, exchange and communication between people, groups and institutions. Public space is the nexus, the scene of intensified contacts, rather characteristic of democracy and the principle of freedom.

"Many of the most difficult environmental challenges of the world can be addressed and solved by cities". (Douglas Foy and Robert Healy)

Urban Sustainability: Dialogue on Ecology, Economy and Society

Spain—Open City is a big square or street, a flexible, versatile and ever changing space, a place where any kind of event can take place, mimicking its exterior and interior image to the rhythm of the various proposed uses and projecting a kaleidoscopic image of a live country.

Technology, Innovation and Creativity

Spain—Open City is a rallying point, a catalyst where reality meets with virtual networks and where virtual communication may have its meeting point and connection to a particular physical space.

Climate Function, Generator of Adjustable and Artificial Breeze

Spain—Open City is a functioning pavilion connected to the reality of the climate of its surroundings, generating varying breezes depending on the weather conditions at every moment, achieving an adaptable and comfortable environment at all times.

Lightweight, Dismountable and Removable

Spain—Open City comprises self-contained, removable and

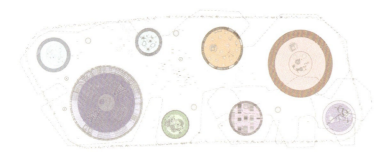

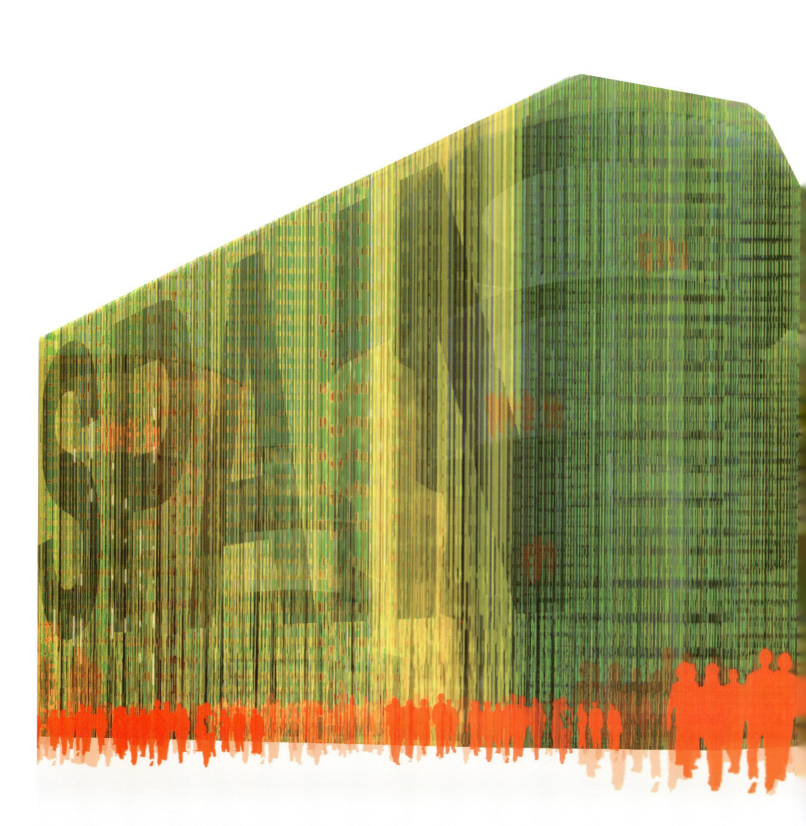

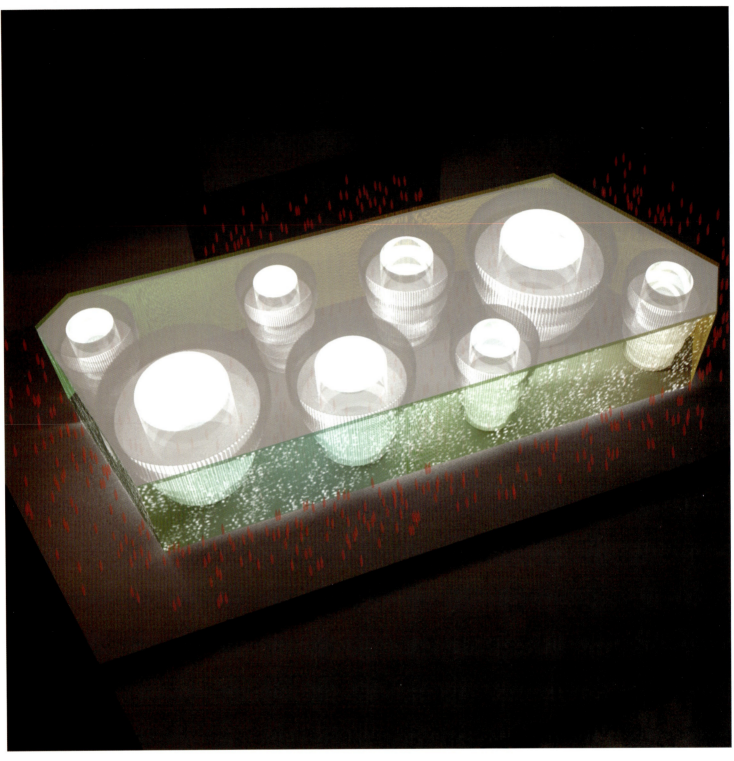

transportable elements, which function individually as catalysts for activities. Once the Shanghai International Exhibition closes, the building could be fragmented and each of its media pavilions could be transported to different Chinese cities, to encourage and promote contacts and knowledge of Spain in different regions of the country.

Shanghai EXPO 2010 Sweden Pavilion Competition

Project name: Sweden Pavilion **Designer:** Sweco Architects **Place in the competition:** Winner **Organiser:** Committee for Sweden's Participation in World EXPO 2010 in Shanghai **Theme:** The Light of Innovation

Project Description:

The Sweden Pavilion expresses the importance of sustainable architecture and innovation. The pavilion uses a holistic approach that is intended to make visitors feel welcome from the moment they join the queue until they leave the pavilion full of new experiences and impressions. The architecture of the pavilion reflects a sustainability perspective in many ways. It can among other things easily be moved and reused.

The Sweden Pavilion at EXPO 2010 is a temporary building that will contain the Swedish exhibition, VIP areas and other facilities such as offices. The 3,000 square metres building will be constructed on a section approximately of the same size, and will be located in the European section alongside other Nordic countries.

The large public exhibition in the pavilion will reflect Sweden and Swedish capability. The VIP section of the pavilion is available for specially invited guests. A programme of different activities will be arranged in this section, including lectures, seminars, film showings, concerts, receptions and dinners. The VIP area will have a large auditorium along with a number of smaller reception rooms. The kitchen will enable Swedish culinary specialties to be prepared for Chinese guests along with a selection of Chinese dishes. The pavilion will also provide office space for pavilion personnel and visiting co-financiers.

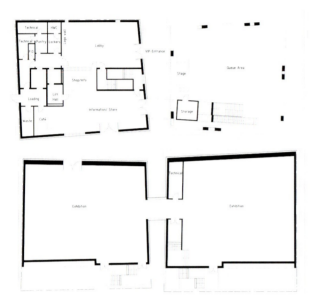

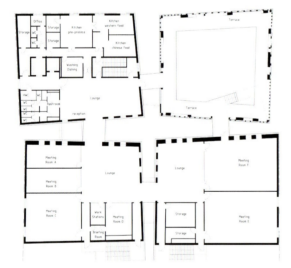

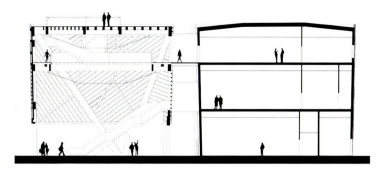

Project name: Switzerland Pavilion **Designer:** Buchner Bründler Architects and Element GmbH **Place in the competition:** Winner **Organiser:** Federal Department of Foreign Affairs, Presence Switzerland **Theme:** The Interaction Between Urban and Rrural Areas

Shanghai EXPO 2010 Switzerland Pavilion Competition

Project Description:

The design of the Switzerland Pavilion is based on the concept of balance rooted in the principle of "Yin and Yang". A vast planted roof and two load-bearing cylinders together make up the structure of the building, and are connected by a revolving chair lift system. The architecture incorporates the symbiosis between town and country, and emphasises the perfect balance of man, nature and technology.

The façade that envelops the pavilion is a curtain of woven aluminium elements with LED lights incorporated. Walking along the three-metre wide ramp, visitors will pass by 3D screens and viewers-60 in all-that have been installed to provide visitors with three-dimensional images of innovative and sustainable Swiss success stories. At the end of the ramp, they will enter the exhibition hall and come across Swiss men and women who represent the diversity of Switzerland and its population, projected on life-size screens against a background of mountain views, recounting their visions of the future, their expectations, and their dreams. After the ramp and the exhibition area, visitors will move into the urban area on the ground floor, where a multifunctional stage, a shop, and a restaurant combine with the urban setting, providing visitors with a sense of what it feels like to be in a bustling city.

After visiting the exhibition, visitors will come to the second cylinder

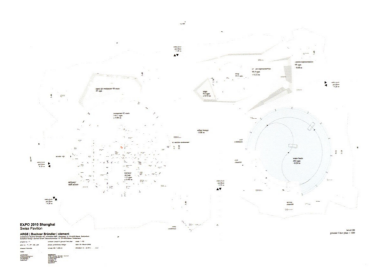

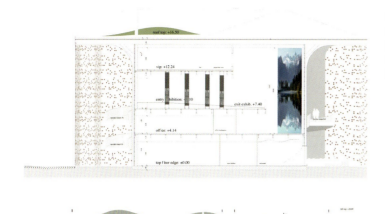

of the Switzerland Pavilion, where they can start the tour on the chair lift. The second cylinder is open at the top and its walls are planted with greenery. The chair lift takes visitors out of the demanding, urban environment into the relaxing rural setting and back again.

Shanghai EXPO 2010 Taiwan Pavilion Competition

Project name: Taiwan Pavilion **Designer:** C.Y.LEE & Partner Architects/Planners **Place in the competition:** Winner **Organiser:** Taipei World Trade Centre **Theme:** Nature, Mind, City

Project Description:

In the 21st century, we are confronted with many problems: environmental protection, anti-nucleus, global crisis, economic crisis, etc. In such a context, the design of the Taiwan Pavilion is to advocate the new idea of "revolution of life". "Nature" and "mind" would be the two elements in this revolution for establishing a new human civilisation in the 21st century. The EXPO 2010 in Shanghai, with the theme of "Better City, Better Life", provides a perfect stage for the practice of this revolution of life.

Taiwan is the inheritor of oriental civilization, and further carries it forward. In western civilisation rational thinking on technology has always been emphasised, while in the east, we advocate the combination of "heaven, earth, and people". From this can be seen the wisdom on life and the concept of a harmonious coexistence. The design of the Taiwan Pavilion adopted this oriental philosophy, and combined it with contemporary advanced technologies to create a new urban civilisation where "nature" and "mind" are highlighted, for the purpose of achieving some sort of a balance in modern society with too much emphasis on technology and consuming.

The design adopted the peculiar folk ceremony of "lighting lamps" in Taiwan, with the connotation of praying for happiness and the purification of mind, to express that in the new urban civilization with the revolution of life, we shall go back to nature and a pure mind.

The configuration of the Taiwan Pavilion is quite eye-catching, with "nature" and "mind" as two subthemes. The huge LED lit lamp-

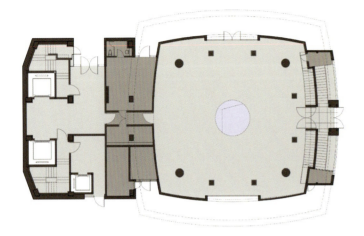

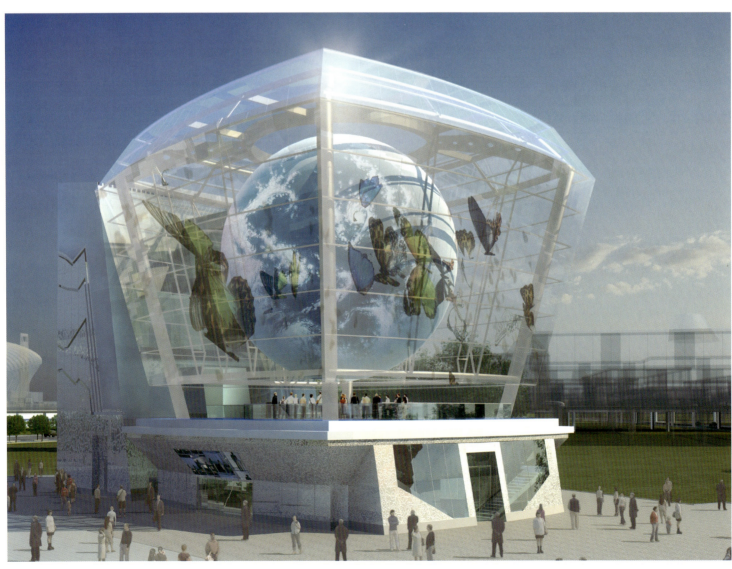

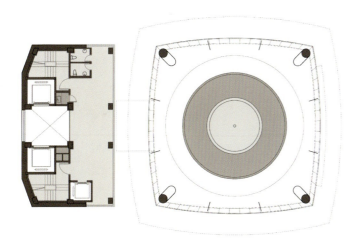

shape architecture is named "the heart of Taiwan", engraved with various artistic images in Taiwan, showing the multi-culture of Taiwan with the 5,000 years history of China, blended with heterogeneous cultures from all over the world. Different sceneries would be presented during day and night. The sparkling "lamp" is a symbol of the role of Taiwan in Shanghai EXPO.

In addition, a theatre is constructed to be the base and the protection of the "lamp". The theatre adopted the metaphor of Yu Mountain in Taiwan and the Pacific Ocean. Performances with specific Taiwan features, natural or cultural, would be put on stage, displaying a life "back to nature" in the future city, illustrating that Taiwan, in the 21st century, would be a perfect resort of the world.

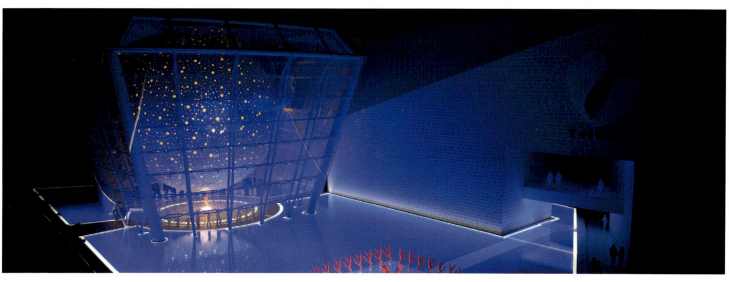

Shanghai 2010 EXPO Centre Competition

Project name: EXPO Centre **Designer:** East China Architectural Design & Research Institute Co., Ltd **(ECADI) Place in the competition:** Winner **Organiser:** Shanghai EXPO 2010 Bureau

Project Description:

The EXPO Centre, as a permanent building, will perform a very important role during and after the EXPO. During the EXPO, she will be used as the centre of operation and direction, celebration and conference, press, forum activity, etc. Meetings of all participating countries and organisers and all kinds of press conferences will be held here. After the EXPO, the centre will be a place for high profile international conferences as well as important domestic forums and meetings, providing first-class conference and service facilities for the whole world. East China Design Institute is in charge of the design of the project, shouldering the responsibilities in terms of the overall coordination and management. Being urgent, complicated, and having many special design units involved, the task has been very demanding for the design team. Therefore, the institute has attached great importance to the project and made lots of efforts including the vigorous participation, of the talented and has achieved a series of fruitful results, in their words, through "upholding the scientific view of development, and being brave to conquer the technical challenges", "introducing the advanced construction materials, and actively conducting the integrated innovation", "implementing the system optimisation, and having a prominent effect in engineering cost saving", "integrating the elites in the institute, and creating a good quality team", "carrying out the field design, and striving to guarantee adequate and systematic services", etc. So far the institute has achieved the following accomplishments, in terms of green architecture and energy efficiency in particular.

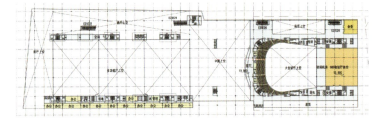

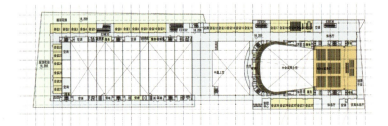

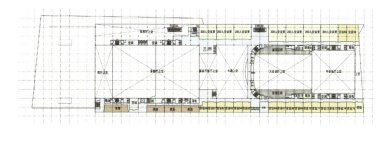

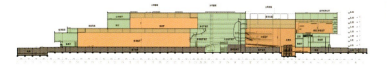

剖面

On National Level
Three-star Rating Identification in Green Architecture Design by the State Ministry of Construction in July 2008
Demonstration Project of Green Construction in the Country (registration and record) by the State Ministry of Construction in December 2007
On the Municipal Level
New Project of Green Construction (registration and record) by the Construction Commission of Shanghai in March 2008
Demonstration Project of Energy Conservation in Building (registration and record) by the Construction Commission of Shanghai in September 2008

INDEX

Tonkin Zulaikha Greer Architects

christian@tzg.com.au

Span Zeytinoglu

sz@info.com

Conix Architects

hbu@conixarchitects.com

Julien De Smedt

jds@jdsa.dk

Studio Performa A+U

studio.performa@fastwebnet.it

John McAslan and Partners

a.stawarz@mcaslan.co.uk

Zaha Hadid

Joann.JoannHong@zaha-hadid.com

Sabbagh Arquitectos

sdelacuadra@sabbagharquitectos.com

HE Jingtang, ZHANG Li, NI Yang

4202036@qq.com

Studio di Architettura Luca Scacchetti

info@scacchetti.com

Kancelář generálního komisaře

kralova@czexpo.com

BIG

info@big.com

MAPT Anders Lendager, Mads Møller with Femmes Regionales, KHR and InnovationLab.

chris@mapt.dk

3XN Architects

lrj@3xn.dk

ARCHITECT BJARKE INGELS GROUP

jm@big.dk

JKMM Architects

eero.kontuniemi@jkmm.fi

Jacques Ferrier Architectures

s.krafft@agencejfa.com

Perioher

afja.peripheriques@club-internet.fr

Rudy Ricciotti

jm.ricciotti@magiconline.fr

Arm

mpetroff@corso70.com

Romain VIAULT / DESUNIQUES

romainviault@yahoo.fr

Schmidhuber + Kaindl GmbH, Munich

m.conrady@koelnmesse.de

Joey Ho Design Ltd

celia@joeyhodesign.com

bomba

bombadiltoma@gmail.com

Mérték Architectural Studio, Hungary

contact@mertek.hu

Urban Landscape Group

szollossy@vtcs.hu

Pall Hjaltason, +ARKITEKTAR, Arnbjorg Haflidadottir, SagaEvents

jon.saemundsson@utn.stjr.is

Office of Public Works

John.Lynam@dfa.ie

Haim Dotan

dotanarc@yahoo.com

Knafo Klimor Architects

haifa@kkarc.com

Giampaolo Imbrighi

studio@iodicearchitetti.it

BiCuadro Architects

info@bicuadro.it

Manfredi Nicoletti

studio.nicoletti@inwind.it

massstudies

info@masstudies.com

Hermann & Valentiny et Associés

Kirchner@hvp.lu

he playze

info@heplayze.com

Marreiros Arquitectos Associados

choipe0601@gmail.com

AS Arquitectura

info@as.com

Serrano Monjaraz Arquitectos

eugenia@circulocuadrado.com.mx

Implementing Experts Group (IEG) of Kathmandu

binayak-shah@hotmail.com

John Kormeling

kormeling@onsneteindhoven.nl

Helen&Hard

ra@hha.no

WWA

info@wwa.com

Ingarden & Ewy Architects, Krakow, Poland

k.ingarden@ingarden-ewy.com.pl

paper team

paperteam@gmail.com

Studio CUBEX

info@cubex.rs

Nikola Arsenic, Ueslei Bonin

nikola@arsenicbonin.com

KAY NGEE TAN ARCHITECTS

kiangsiew@kayngeetanarchitects.com

EMBT

mfornells@mirallestagliabue.com

ecosistema urbano

michael@ecosistemaurbano.com

Sweco Architects

Rebecka.gunner@sweco.se

Buchner & Bründler Architects

poorfanfan@hotmail.com

C.Y.LEE&PARTNER ARCHITECTS/PLANNERS

chiuanne@mail.cylee.com

ECADI

zjzj@ecadi.com

GREAT VISION FOR FUTURE – WORLD EXPO 2010 SHANGHAI
Copyright © 2010 by Liaoning Science and Technology Publishing House

Published in Asia in (year) by
Page One Publishing Pte Ltd
20 Kaki Bukit View
Kaki Bukit Techpark II
Singapore 415956
Tel: [65] 6742-2088
Fax: [65] 6744-2088
enquiries@pageonegroup.com
www.pageonegroup.com

First published 2010 by Liaoning Science and Technology Publishing House

Chief Editor: Chen Cilang
Cover Designer: Li Ning
Layout Designer: Li Ning

ISBN 978-981-245-911-4

Printed in China